To Joe
from Fred.

In memory of
the eventful years

THE MOST DANGEROUS MOMENT

THE
MOST DANGEROUS
MOMENT

Michael Tomlinson

WILLIAM KIMBER · LONDON

First published in 1976 by
WILLIAM KIMBER & CO. LIMITED
Godolphin House, 22a Queen Anne's Gate,
London, SW1H 9AE

© Michael Tomlinson, 1976
ISBN 0 7183 0434 9

Filmset by
Input Typesetting Ltd., London
and printed in Great Britain by
The Pitman Press, Bath

'He considered the most dangerous moment of the war, and the one which caused him the greatest alarm, was when the news was received that the Japanese Fleet was heading for Ceylon and the naval base there.'

LESTER PEARSON
speaking of Winston Churchill

Contents

A map of the area of operations
appears on Pages 48–9

List of Illustrations

The author would like to thank all those who so kindly supplied him with illustrations for this book, including the late Captain Augustus Agar, VC, Squadron-Leader Brian Catlin, Squadron-Leader Charles Gardner, OBE, the Department of the Air Force, United States, Captain R. A. Lushington and Mr. E. M. Thomas

Foreword

by
Air Chief Marshal Sir Peter Fletcher
KCB, OBE, DFC, AFC

When Michael Tomlinson told me that he was writing this book my first reaction was one of mixed feelings. On the one hand I was pleased because I had long felt that too little was known about the operations over and around Ceylon. Apart from the effect they could have had, and perhaps did have, on the course of the war as a whole this was a brief period of time richly packed with incident, human experience and material of value to students of strategy. On the other hand I had two fears. The first was that many books have been written about operations and experiences during the 1939–45 war and some of those dealing with situations of which I had personal experience or professional knowledge seemed to illustrate only too well how difficult it can be to paint a true picture on the canvas of war, particularly in terms of assessing how the people involved discharged their responsibilities, and my fear was that the Ceylon story might fall into this category because there were a number of hitherto unanswered questions and also some events that were difficult to interpret. My second fear was whether, after such a long passage of time, the author could trace sufficient sources of information and also, a selfish thought perhaps, would I in due course read a book that struck a jarring note in relation to the experiences so vividly etched on my memory?

I soon realised that my fears were groundless. With almost incredible patience and determination Michael Tomlinson had devoted years of effort to research in depth and detail. As a result of this, coupled with his exploration of many people's memories and his own knowledge of Ceylon, he has produced not only a very interesting and readable story but also a documentary contribution to the history of the war that both captures the atmosphere of those dangerous times and contains much information not previously available.

For me, reading a book dealing with events that occurred so much earlier in my life has been a strange experience. It revived some memories that had faded with the passing of time: it revived the feelings, anxieties and uncertainties that those of us who were there lived through: it also revealed the fallibility of some beliefs and judgements. Among all these was my pride in my 'international' squadron and my sadness when some of them lost their lives. Another was my belief, shared by many when the battles were over, that the Japanese would return and because of the state of our defences my anxiety that the island would prove an easy prey. Yet another, again shared by many of whom some were in very high places, was my belief that the Japanese had suffered a reverse and on this I think there is still some room for debate. In the first place the enemy sank some ships but did not achieve his objective of finding and destroying the British fleet, although we cannot claim that the air battles were responsible for the avoidance of that disaster. In the second place, as far as the air battles were concerned, judgement on whether to claim victory or admit defeat is not simply a matter of arithmetic in comparing the losses suffered by both sides. Apart from the fact that there remains some doubt as to what the Japanese losses actually were, the widely held view that the Ceylon operations had deflected the enemy from continuing with his original strategic plans gave a boost to the Allied cause at a time when one was sorely needed.

This book is dedicated to the many who took part in operations in the Indian Ocean in March, April and May 1942 and, more especially, to those who died in those waters, on the surrounding shores or in the neighbouring skies. It recalls too the days when we were all of us in it together – Canadians, South Africans, New Zealanders, Rhodesians, Indians, Dutchmen, Ceylonese, Australians and (of necessity on the sidelines of this particular sphere of operations) Americans. Yet, lest it be forgotten, the greatest number on the Allied side were English, plain and simple, with the usual heavy leavening of Scots and Welsh. Irishmen there will have been too, of course.

Whether one wishes it or not this book cannot fail to pay a like tribute to the enormous efficiency and fighting spirit of the Japanese who opposed them.

Preface

Ask the average young man of 25 or so a few random questions on World War II. Even though his father may well have fought in it, the result is likely to be chastening.

Hitler and Churchill he has certainly heard of. Probably Mussolini and Tojo too. Rommel, Wavell, Zhukov and Yamamoto may, or may not, ring a bell. Hiroshima he knows about but probably not Nagasaki. The Battle of Britain, Stalingrad and Pearl Harbour have secured too firm a position in history to be gainsaid. But Kohima, Iwojima, Cassino and the Battle of the Bulge – what does he know of these?

One may sympathise if he is little informed about all this. How can he equate it all with the world he lives in? True, it has never been a peaceful world but to-day only the merest fraction of western youth has seen war first hand. Most have been brought up to the theme 'Make love, not war'; they know the futility and appalling waste of warfare. They have decided that the very idea is all wrong – an affront to humanity, a denial of civilisation and progress.

The previous generation who served in the last world war would certainly have seen the sense of this. It would be effrontery to think otherwise; even more so our grandfathers whose generation fought World War I, secure in the knowledge that it was the War--to-End-War. But they would surely have seen it as a naive and im-practicable creed. Whatever their religious up-bringing might have been, 'The meek shall inherit the earth' was something to which they could not give full credence. There would always be someone to bank on and take every advantage of open and vaunted pacifism. To them war was certainly vicious and wasteful but they saw that with the best will in the world it could become a regrettable necessity.

Talk to any man old enough to have gone off to either of the World Wars and he will readily fall back on a mass of recollections; things that will never be forgotten, though the years have largely shorn them of bitterness. New horizons, a break in the ordered pattern of a humdrum existence; courage and comradeship, hardships and tragedy; the discipline, the tedium and the useless sacrifice.

In either of the two struggles, to be numbered amongst the countless war dead, whatever the manner of it, was to have made a noble sacrifice. To those who made this sacrifice it was never vouchsafed whether they died in vain or not – mercifully perhaps for the vanquished; more poignantly for men who perished in a cause that ultimately triumphed.

To have fought through a Malta convoy, to have been a Kamikaze flyer, to have landed on the Normandy beaches on D-Day, to have hung on tenaciously at Stalingrad, to have died in aerial combat in the Battle of Britain or at Midway, was to be ensured, collectively if not individually, an established place in history and enduring recognition. But many died needlessly in operations which failed or were pointless or brought no worthwhile strategic gain. Fighting rearguard actions in out of the way places. Or not fighting at all, for that matter; lives being simply lost with nothing to show for it. For the first three years of the Second World War there was far too much of this on the Allied side. Poles and Czechs who saw their countries over-run, Canadians in the Dieppe raid, British troops in France, Norway, Crete, Singapore and Dunkirk will always be remembered, but how much else of these profitless ventures?

This book has been written in an attempt to bring into the light a brief chapter of the war which, to the writer's astonishment, seems so far to have escaped narration, except in the most cursory way. Looking back a whole generation later with the vast comprehensive strategic sweep of the war before us events fall easily into their proper place. We now know that the operations dealt with here neither much hastened defeat or ultimate victory, nor led to irreparable losses or material gains to either side. But, safe in the comfortable reassurance which hindsight affords us, it is only too easy to overlook the enormous importance which was attached to these events at the time or to underrate the consternation and gloom which prevailed in the British camp as the Japanese swept ever westwards and there seemed no holding them.

The full measure of alarm at the furthest incursion westwards which the Japanese were ever to make by land, sea or air, with all its trenchant and catastrophic possibilities, has since been demonstrated, as the book will show, by no less a figure than the arbiter of British survival and ultimate victory, Sir Winston Churchill, and in unmistakeably forceful terms.

In the space of a week or so, in early April 1942, a thousand lives were lost – mainly British. The threat receded and we breathed again.

Historians have touched only briefly and generally obliquely on the Japanese Navy's only major offensive westwards. Small wonder that our 25-year-old will never have heard of 'The April Raids' as Ceylon remembers them for history itself has almost forgotten them.

Because Churchill has told us he considered the moment so dangerous to our cause and because, in Sir Arthur Bryant's words, a Japanese naval victory in April 1942 'would have given Japan control of the Indian Ocean, isolated the Middle East *and brought down the Churchill Government*' [1] (the italics are mine) I feel I have the necessary justification for filling in the definite gap which others have left, having been personally involved, albeit on the periphery only, in this little known chapter of the last world war. Because of the prolific documentation already collected on the Second World War in its widest phases, one has to produce a plausible excuse for adding to it at this late stage. One can also cite the generally held notion that time confers better historical perspective. Old animosities, too, have had time to cool during the ensuing thirty odd years.

I have drawn to some extent on the works of other writers and am glad to acknowledge here the debt I owe them. The list of their works is fairly short and appears in the Bibliography.

[1] The Turn of the Tide, William Collins.

Much, however, is taken from first hand accounts provided over the years by many people, now spread over the four corners of the world. Almost none of these have been previously published.

To the late Mr Lester Pearson I am indebted for his invaluable quotation of Sir Winston Churchill which has added much point to my narrative. In addition I have to record my gratitude and appreciation for their accounts and for their considerable help in other ways to the following:

On the Naval side.
Captain Augustus Agar, VC, RN, His Honour Judge (Commander) L. K. A. Block, DSC, DL, Commander T. L. M. Brander, DSC, RN, Lieutenant D. P. P. Brimble, RNVR, Commander G. M. T. Grove, DSC, RN, Lieutenant R. V. Hinton, RNVR, Lieutenant Duncan Kennedy, RSAN, Able Seaman R. Lock, Commander S. M. de L. Longsdon, RN and Captain J. Milner, OBE, RN.

On the Air Force side.
Air Commodore L. J. Birchall, OBE, DFC, RCAF, Squadron Leader Brian Catlin, RAF, Air Chief Marshal Sir Peter Fletcher, KCB, OBE, DFC, AFC, Wing Commander D. H. T. Hildyard, CMG, DSO, Flight Lieutenant Charles Gardner, RAFVR, Marshal of the RAF Sir Arthur Harris, GCB, OBE, AFC, Flight Lieutenant J. L. Loam, RAFVR, Squadron Leader S. R. Peacock-Edwards, DFC, RAF and Mr. E. M. Thomas.

The officials of the Air Historical Branch of the Ministry of Defence have also been most helpful in permitting access to squadron records etc. To them and to Mrs. R. E. Dolphin (now Mrs. Michael Tomlinson) who did most of the research, my thanks are due.

I am required to make it clear that any views or observations relating to this material are those of the author alone and do not reflect official views held by the Ministry of Defence.

From Japan.
Admiral Takaichi Itaya, Lieutenant-Colonel Kyushiro Kewada, Commander Eiziro Suzuki and Miss Etsuko Watanabe.

From Ceylon.

Dr Colvin R. de Silva, Mr Rodney S. L. Jonklaas, B.Sc. and Captain R. H. Salvador, C. L. I., Captain R. A. Lushington, 1st Punjab Regiment.

The island known to the author as Ceylon during his twenty seven years there is now of course officially Sri Lanka which, in Singhalese, means Blessed (or Respected) Island. To the Ceylonese it was always Lanka; so it is only to the outside world that the new name has had much significance.

Known in olden times to the Arabs as Serendib and later to the Greeks and others as Taprobane, the island seems to have received its renomination at the hands of the Portuguese, who used the name Ceilao. The Dutch version of this was Zeilan and the British, Ceylon.

For all purposes throughout this book I shall use this name. It was current during the whole period of which I am writing and Ceylon will always be remembered as such by the countless soldiers, sailors and airmen who served there or merely passed through during the last War. It is perhaps worth noting here that, economic factors being so important, we are not yet exhorted to 'Buy Sri Lanka Tea'.

Japanese Names.

To suit Western readers Japanese given names have been placed before surnames in reversal of the Japanese custom.

A Note on Times.

In order to give a clearer picture of events, all times quoted are local times. In point of fact ships at sea, as well as long range reconnaissance aircraft, kept their logs etc. in Z time (G. M. T.) and the Japanese Navy adhered to Tokyo time. All these have been converted to the time in force in the appropriate area. As far as the Ceylon operations were concerned, this was Indian Standard Time.

Newlands,
Cape Town.
19th March 1976

Prologue and Epilogue

In March 1946, a few months after the final triumphant termination of the Second World War, with the congratulations of the Free World ringing in his ears, though the Premiership of the United Kingdom had been newly wrested from him by an unexpectedly ungrateful electorate, Sir Winston Churchill was the chief guest at a dinner at the British Embassy in Washington. This visit to the United States is chiefly memorable for Sir Winston's address at Fulton University, Missouri, in which he first coined the term 'the Iron Curtain'. His host was the British Ambassador to the United States, Lord Halifax.

Over coffee, cigars and port, the conversation turned to the critical moments of the struggle which had just ended. Someone asked Sir Winston what he felt to be the most dangerous and the most distressing moment of the War. Mr Lester Pearson, later Prime Minister of Canada, and then Canadian Ambassador, recalls: 'Most of us thought he would refer to the events of June and July 1940 and the imminence of invasion by Germany; or to the time when Rommel was heading towards Alexandria and Cairo at full speed; or when Singapore fell.'

But none of these incidents sprang to Churchill's mind as his listeners tensely awaited the great man's reply.

'He considered the most dangerous moment of the War,' he said, 'and the one which caused him the greatest alarm, was when the news was received that the Japanese Fleet was heading for Ceylon and the naval base there. The capture of Ceylon,' he said, 'the consequent control of the Indian Ocean, and the possibility at the same time of a German conquest of Egypt would have closed the ring and the future would have been black.

'However,' he went on to say, 'we were saved from this disaster by an airman on reconnaissance who spotted the Japanese Fleet and, though shot down, was able to get a message through to Ceylon which allowed the defence forces there to prepare for the approaching assault; otherwise they would have been taken by surprise.'

According to Mr Lester Pearson: 'Sir Winston went on very dramatically to say that the unknown airman, who lay deep in the waters of the Indian Ocean, had made one of the most important single contributions to victory. He got quite emotional about it.'

It is strange that this incident, which Sir Winston Churchill deemed to be of such crucial importance has received so little notice from historians. Even those who have chronicled the war against Japan have given scant recognition to the stirring events which Churchill, if no one else, regarded as a turning point in the war.

What did happen? And where? And when?

How far west did the Japanese Fleet penetrate? And was the course of the War altered as Sir Winston suggests it was?

Who was the unknown airman?

These are some of the questions to be answered in this book and to receive the consideration they deserve.

CHAPTER ONE

Flare-up in the East

'They have attacked us at Pearl Harbour. We are all in
the same boat now.'

FRANKLIN D. ROOSEVELT

To the simple question: 'What, above all, made possible our ultimate triumph against the Axis and Japan in World War II?' there is a simple answer.

Victory might never have been won if Hitler had not been mad enough to attack Russia, who then changed sides, and if Japan had not been mad enough to attack the United States of America, who then became fully combatant and not merely an active sympathiser with the cause of Britain and the few Allies who remained to her once France had fallen.

These two steps by Hitler and Tojo were decisive.

The war in Europe does not concern us here, but it is worth considering why Japan, a small semi-industrial Asiatic country, ambitious though she was for expansion, should ever have considered crossing swords with a country now, if not then, recognised as one of the World's two major Powers.

But the fact is she had done the very same thing before, and with complete success.

Although entirely withdrawn from the rest of the world until the middle of the 19th Century, once her horizons had widened, Japan, under the relentless pressure of an ever expanding population was quick to foster ambitions to spread herself at the expense of her neighbours. Such acquisitions of territory seemed to be a logical and proper part of the natural order of things, for every Japanese was moved by an unshakeable belief that his Emperors – indeed all Japanese – were descended from the Sun Goddess and were therefore divine beings. They were not however averse to an undisguised admiration for such western ideas as seemed worth adopting and to the slavish copying and reproduction of much of the myriad material products of western technology. In 1942 no-one foresaw that she would soon cease merely to copy but would in many instances carry production and development appreciably further than the originators had done.

Even before the close of the 19th Century Japan had annexed outlying islands and territories such as the Kuriles, Okinawa and Formosa and in 1904 her expansion through Korea, considered intolerable by the Russians (and by other Powers too), had brought the two countries to blows. When Japan began the Russo-Japanese War of 1904–5 with the first Asian army and navy to be organised and equipped on modern lines she seems to have had behind her the admiration and moral support of many Western nations. Hardened veterans, as it were, were generous in their encouragement of an untried young knight, with his spurs freshly won under their tutelage.

In the popular view the Russo-Japanese War had a David and Goliath element about it and, somewhat to everyone's surprise, Admiral Heihachiro Togo proceeded to annihilate a large Russian Fleet in the Tsushima Strait, between Korea and Japan. Russia at that time was certainly one of the largest powers in the World and the tonnage sunk, with almost trifling loss to the Japanese, remains the highest in history to be sunk in a single battle.

In that earlier war, which would still have been within the memories of many Japanese in 1941, the initial attack by Togo on the Russian fleet at Port Arthur had been made, just as it would be at Pearl Harbour, without a prior declaration of war. Though it was planned that war against the United States would have been declared just before the attack fell upon the Americans it obviously seemed to the Japanese in 1941 that history could be repeated.

After World War I, which Japan had entered on the Allied side, the major naval powers had joined in a number of pacts designed to limit naval armaments by means of a formula which as far as possible would both afford the signatories reasonable defence against aggression and prevent any one power from building a fleet to threaten its neighbours. At the Washington Naval Conference of 1921 Japan had accepted this formula which limited her navy to 6/10ths of the strength of either the British or American fleets. This formula was in reality much to her advantage for she was involved only in the Pacific whereas Britain (to a very great extent) and the USA (to a less extent) had heavy naval commitments in other theatres. Even so at the subsequent London Naval Conference in 1930 Japan expressed dissatisfaction with this limitation and the new London Treaty left her on a slightly better basis vis-a-vis both Britain and America. Neither of the latter governments, preoccupied with the crippling economic crisis of those times, had any desire to increase expenditure on armaments and it was mainly through their forbearance to build ships up to treaty limits that Japan was accorded some additional advantage. It had been part of the terms of the 1921 Washington Treaty that neither western power would build heavy land defences in Asia.

By 1935, at the Second London Naval Conference, when the time came to review the treaty obligations, Japan had set her sights on building a large autonomous empire in Eastern Asia under her suzerainty. She now sought parity with both Britain and the USA in naval armaments and would settle for no less. The implications were fairly clear, for Japan was already heavily involved in Northern China though she had not yet openly taken up arms there. America was still unwilling to enter into an arms race with Japan and Britain was more concerned with the threat to European peace which Hitler was posing at this time. In both countries to advocate heavy expenditure on armaments was deemed political suicide. Stanley Baldwin had just been elected Prime Minister by an electorate much attuned to disarmament and Franklin D. Roosevelt was about to embark on a presidential campaign which would return him to power for a second term. As an ex-Secretary for the Navy he recognised as well as anyone the threat which Japan's attitude now posed and understood that it was aimed primarily at the USA, but he was well aware that a compulsive isolationism gripped a large and significant element of the American people who could not be ignored.

Because of this isolationism, American reaction to the forceful occupation of Manchuria had been restricted to bolstering the League of Nations, of which the USA itself was not a member, into bringing economic pressure against Japan. This had little effect and Japan merely resigned from the League.

So strong was this spirit of isolationism in the USA that

throughout the late 1930s when Hitler and Mussolini were making their determinedly aggressive movements in Europe, President Roosevelt, though alive as few of his countrymen were to the threat to world security which the totalitarian powers were posing, was quite unable to make any counter-move in concert with Britain or any of the European nations for fear of being thought a mere accessory to the colonial ambitions of the Imperialist powers, particularly those of Britain.

When in December 1937 the American gunboat *Panay* was sunk by Japanese bombing in the Yangtse river and Jap field batteries much damaged HMS *Ladybird,* Roosevelt went to extraordinary lengths not to concert his protests with those of the British Government.

The Japanese were not slow to note this.

Early in 1936 when it was clear that they could not attain their aims by negotiation the Japanese withdrew from the London Naval Conference, abrogated the Treaty and declined to co-operate by making public their future building programme. Henceforward whilst other nations would continue to observe armaments limitations laid down by the new London Naval Treaty Japan would ignore these and would construct battleships with guns of a much larger calibre than those allowed to signatories of the new treaty.

Generally speaking Japan set much store by her navy at this time in contrast to both Britain and the USA whose governments were wedded to the maintenance of a peaceful status quo. The Japanese were highly successful in concealing the build-up of their fleet from the West, where some complacency inevitably tempered apprehension over Japanese ambitions.

Noteworthy too was the considerable political power wielded by naval and military circles in Japan. This was out of all proportion to the modest influence which Service chiefs customarily enjoyed in Europe or America.

In 1937 the long, cruel struggle for the domination of China, euphemistically termed in Japan 'The China Incident' developed into open warfare, though never declared as such. By the time of Pearl Harbour the fighting had been going on for four years (and would still have a further four years to go).

Throughout their aggression in northern China the Japanese were able to fob off individual diplomatic protests with mildly phrased apologies, vague statements of peaceful intentions, bogus complaints against China and so on. Though American opinion was gradually won over it was not until Pearl Harbour, which instantly unified the entire nation, that Roosevelt felt constrained, without fear of opposition, to align the USA firmly with Great Britain in Asia, as in Europe, against the Tripartite Powers.

However, on the outbreak of war in Europe the Americans, unable any longer to ignore the challenge in the Pacific, began to respond; re-arming with the full range of their massive resources and recognising that Britain's occupation with the war in Europe, left responsibility for the Pacific theatre almost exclusively in American hands.

Japan was not invulnerable. She possessed no sources of oil, the life blood of any industrial nation. And the United States was her supplier. In July 1940 the President had been granted by Congress valuable powers to restrict the export of all potential war material. He promptly began to use these powers and Japan was refused iron, steel, fuel oil, aircraft spares, many chemicals and other items. A year later, less than six months before Pearl Harbour, all Japanese assets in the United States, Great Britain and the Netherlands were frozen. Though Japan retaliated in kind it was clear that she was now held in an economic stranglehold. The USA made it clear that complete withdrawal from China was the price demanded for relaxation of the controls.

Prince Konoye's moderate government gave some consideration to withdrawal from China. But War Minister General Hideki Tojo and the strong military element which supported him would not hear of it. Warlike councils prevailed, Konoye resigned and Tojo took over the Premiership. He had no difficulty in carrying the Emperor and the Cabinet with him and the decision was made for war unless the Americans would appreciably modify their stand.

Negotiations were still under way in Washington when, as the world knows, the Japanese Navy struck at Hawaii.

These facts are worth recalling, and perhaps underlining. For the widely held belief still exists that America was attacked for reasons only of Japanese greed, perfidy and jealousy. As they saw it, to secure essential raw materials, of which there were plenty in South East Asia, to save the very life of their Empire, the Japanese now had to resort to arms. Japan had been put in a position in which she had to make the choice, furthermore, between a heavy diplomatic defeat, with a temporary check to her expansionist ambitions, accompanied by grievous loss of face – or war.

By 1941, therefore, Russia had lost her traditional place as Japan's main rival in the East. She had held this place since the beginning of the century but now the United States of America had largely supplanted her as the villain of the piece. Although Japanese and Russian troops had actually clashed on the Manchurian border, the Russians were not considered such a stumbling block to Japanese expansion in Asia as the Americans. The USA had made their position perfectly clear and had taken the firmest line on this, backing up their warnings with economic measures which threatened Japan's very existence.

This did not mean that Russia could be forgotten.

The Japanese knew perfectly well that they could not align themselves against both Russia and America with any hope of success. But by November 1941 the prospects of German victory in Russia seemed excellent and had much to do with the timing of Japanese offensive operations.

Thus the Imperial High Command firmly believed that Japan, after the swift destruction of the American Pacific Fleet, could bludgeon America into withdrawing her support for Nationalist China, could secure oil and other raw materials from the Netherlands East Indies, Malaya, Borneo and Burma and, while Germany disposed of Britain and Russia as effective forces, continue her subjugation of China.

Though each pursuing their own separate ends, Hitler and the Japanese leaders both found themselves with a similar problem and both, in the end, were to be overwhelmed by the actions of the other.

Neither could afford to take on the United States and Russia together.

Stalin in Russia had hoped to play a waiting game. He would keep Russia out of the struggle, wait aloof on the sidelines and then take advantage of the disorganisation and destruction which the warring Western Powers would inevitably bring down on Europe. The Russian signing of the Moscow Pact in August 1939, a complete volte face for both Russia and Germany which caused much embarrassment to each country as well as to Communists throughout the world, ensured for Hitler the safety of his rear while he dealt with France and Great Britain. But Stalin's reasons for the Pact were much more cynical. He made certain that the Second World War would be fought. If he had aligned Russia with Britain and France, as both countries strove to get him to do, there was every chance that the War might be averted. That was not in Russia's interests. Nor was it in Russia's interest to have to take part in the War. In one fell swoop the Pact enlarged Russia's western territories almost bloodlessly, sparked off the War and, as Stalin thought, kept Russia out of the struggle.

To Japan, aligned with Germany, the Moscow Pact came as a great shock. She found herself unexpectedly in the same camp as her traditional enemy, Russia. But it was soon realised that there were enormous advantages. Just as Hitler could now deal safely with France and Great Britain, Japan could now declare war on the United States with little fear of Russian participation. In April 1941, perhaps in anticipation of Hitler's next move, Japan went further and concluded her own Soviet-Japanese Non-Aggression Pact in Moscow, the terms of which were to be observed until after the dropping of the first atomic bomb on Hiroshima, when the Soviets swiftly declared war on Japan in order to be in at the kill and the division of the spoils.

Thus in April 1941 Soviet Russia was on ostensibly friendly terms with Germany, who had to all intents and purposes brought the War in the West to a successful conclusion, and with Japan, who thus saw herself as ready to sweep aside American interests in Asia and the Pacific.

By the end of the year, however, the position had been transformed.

In June the Germans swept through Russian-held Polish territory and assaulted Soviet-Russia itself. By the end of the year it seemed more than probable that she would beat Russia to her knees (with what consequences one wonders?). Japan had not been consulted, but found with relief that Russia had reiterated her intention of abiding by the terms of their non-aggression pact. If Stalin had taken a different line he might even have averted American entry into the War, for Japan would have had to think again. But Russia could not possibly risk a combined onslaught from the East as well as from the West and had no real choice in the matter.

The Japanese High Command were only too well aware that once an arms race with the United States had been allowed to develop they could not fail, in the long run, to be bested. With every year that passed the advantages which Japan had won since their abrogation of the London Naval Treaty would be whittled away. Russia, Britain, France and Holland were preoccupied with the War in Europe, leaving only the Americans to dispute Japan's long planned expansion. Thus everything pointed to haste. This was the moment to strike. The nettle must be firmly grasped while the balance of circumstances favoured Japan or her dreams of imperialism be abandoned.

On 7th December 1941, Japan, without consulting Germany, struck at Pearl Harbour. The war was now indeed a world war.

If Roosevelt had felt any temptation to make America's entry into the war in any way selective, which is extremely unlikely, he was given no chance to name the chosen belligerents. Matters were taken out of his hands when both Germany and Italy, after a brief delay to concert their actions, themselves declared war on the USA. They had been subjected to some recent pressure by Japan to support her in the event of hostilities though they had been given no inkling at all of Japanese plans to strike immediately at the American Fleet. It was to be the last nail in Germany's coffin and was to greatly undermine such little trust and co-operation as had existed between her and Japan. For Japan, uninvited, had provided the nail; and the hammer as well.

Hitler had, with perhaps less certainty, performed a similar function for Japan by attacking, without their prior knowledge his ally Russia. For although this did not align Soviet Russia against Japan, it immeasurably strengthened the Allies, drawing them much more closely together and at the same time encouraged Japan to embark on a war from which, with Russian hands free, she might have drawn back.

The war in Asia did not begin for Japan, as it did for the USA and Great Britain on 7th December 1941. 'The China Incident' had begun on 7th July 1937. After the fall of France in June 1940, and before de Gaulle's Free French movement possessed any significant forces, let alone Allied recognition, the Japanese walked into French Indo-China. They did so at the invitation of the French Governor-General, Admiral Decoux, on instructions from the Vichy Government who had presumably been prodded in turn into the move by the Germans, Japan's allies, with Italy, in the Tripartite Pact of December 1937. With Germany now in full control of the northern and western areas of France, Vichy's published reasons for admitting the Japanese were to prevent the country's occupation by China, Britain or the Free French and the result of the move was to place Japan in a position to facilitate her oppression of China and her planned conquests of Malaya and Burma.

Three aerodromes were occupied as well as several harbours. Decoux had replaced General Catroux as Governor-General of Indo-China on the defeat of France by Germany. He was to remain in nominal and somewhat ambiguous office throughout the Japanese occupation until, in March 1945, with France liberated and the Vichy Government eclipsed, Japan found the arrangement altogether too tenuous. After a brief and bitter struggle between Japanese and French forces Decoux was arrested whilst his compatriots were compelled to retreat to China.

At the time of the occupation of the peninsula by Japanese forces in September 1940 Britain herself was obliged to yield to demands for the closure of the Burma Road, a tenuous track along which had gone such precious materials and supplies as the Western world was mustering in aid of the Chinese. For this blatant gesture of appeasement there was no reciprocal benefit whatsoever. In Europe the excuse had always been valid that the appeasement of Germany was postponing the hour of trial and allowing a breathing space in which to arm and prepare. Not even this advantage could be claimed for the suspension of aid to the Chungking Government and after three months, in October 1940, convoys ran once again along the Burma Road and Japanese objections were firmly brushed aside.

Though it could scarcely be laid at Vichy France's door, a later result of the eclipse of the French in Indo-China was to be the War in Vietnam, almost certainly the most unpopular war in the whole of recorded history. For by the end of World War II the French had lost every vestige of control in Indo-China; nor were the indigenous peoples of Vietnam, Cambodia and Laos anxious to see them return. American influence, by this time extremely powerful, was of the same opinion. President Roosevelt made no bones about it. He did not wish to see the colonialist powers re-occupying the territories won back from the Japanese in Asia. He envisaged in their place sound, nationalist, democratic governments who would lean towards the USA in gratitude for their liberation. The last thing he would have wished to see supplanting the French was Communism. This was far worse in American eyes than the old Colonialism. It was because the Communists were quick to seize their opportunities that the question of who was to fill the vacuum left so long ago by the departing Japanese was not to be decided until 1975, after an expenditure of American lives and material on an enormous and, as it transpired, fruitless scale.

For all but the Japanese and Chinese the war in the East had blazed up with the most spectacular and successful bombing raid which, until that Sunday morning, 7th December 1941, the world had ever seen. Once or twice in Western Europe over the next eighteen months results almost as spectacular were to be claimed, but until atom bombs were dropped on Hiroshima and Nagasaki, Pearl Harbour stood on its own, a supreme justification for those who had long claimed that air power was being under-estimated.

True the attack was unleashed without a declaration of war and has thus been stamped as an act of infamy, though the Americans had very solid reasons for expecting it and the enormous surprise which the Japanese managed to achieve over the Americans was quite unexpected by their own flyers. Sadly enough when these same airmen, almost man for man the same, were to attack targets in Ceylon four months later, the British, though having extremely accurate and complete intelligence of the Japanese intentions and movements, were taken only a little less by surprise than were the Americans at Hawaii.

This element of surprise was a crucial factor on both occasions and, combined with the experience and extreme efficiency of the Japanese airmen, proved more than a match for the Allied defences.

In December 1941 our information about the Japanese Navy and Army Air Forces was sparse indeed. Considering that they had been in action in one way or another for over four years over China, it is hard to see why. A Japanese writer, Masutake Okumiya, a former flying officer in the Japanese Navy, writes [1]

> Our Navy's chief training grounds were not in the homeland, but far out at sea where even our own people remained unaware of the true extent of air-sea manoeuvres. Further, we concealed in every possible fashion the particulars of our military weapons and especially the performance of our aircraft. Foreign observers saw only what we allowed them to see.
>
> So effective was our armaments censorship that prior to the Pearl Harbour attack not a single American publication realised the existence of the Zero fighter, and not until several months following the opening of hostilities did the American public receive even a reasonably accurate impression of this aeroplane.

It was not only the American public who were so ill informed. American and British Intelligence knew as little. The RAF had only particulars of the older Japanese planes and were referred to German and Italian models of which the Japanese had purchased a few. It was implied that we might meet copies of these. In the official RAF History the following apologia appears in explanation of our complete lack of information about the Zero fighter:

> The Japanese had made use of the Navy Zero against the Chinese in the spring of 1940. Some details of its performance had been divulged by American newspaper correspondents stationed in Chungking, who had seen it in action at that time, and in the same year more details had reached the Air Ministry from other sources in that city. On 2nd September 1941 this information was duly forwarded to the Far Eastern Combined

[1] *Zero!* E. P. Dutton & Co., New York (1957).

Vice-Admiral Chuichi Nagumo, who commanded the First Air Striking Force.

Vice-Admiral Jisabura Ozawa, who commanded the Malaya Force.

Admiral Sir James Somerville, C-in-C Eastern Fleet.

Admiral Sir Geoffrey Layton, C-in-C Ceylon.

Squadron-Leader Birchall in the cockpit of the ill-fated Catalina.

Sergeant Brian Catlin, one of the 41 Squadron airmen to be taken prisoner by the Japanese.

A Catalina flying-boat beneath camouflage netting in Koggala lagoon.

Bureau for transmission to Air Headquarters. It never arrived there. Moreover in addition to the information on this fighter provided by the Air Ministry, a detailed description of it, written in Chinese, reached Singapore in July and was duly transcribed; what happened next is a matter for conjecture, since all records have been destroyed, but it seems probable that this very important report formed part of the mass of accumulated files with which the makeshift Intelligence Section, set up at Air Headquarters in 1941, attempted to deal. When War broke out they had by no means completed their task and the report remained undiscovered.

The Zero proved one of the greatest surprises of the campaign. Fast, well armed and extremely manoeuvrable, it was more than a match for our fighters whose pilots, unaware of its high performance, suffered many casualties through adopting the wrong tactics against it.

The lack of knowledge of both American and British Intelligence about all the latest Japanese aircraft was to be a great handicap to the navies and air forces of both countries. In particular the range and endurance of these planes were to cause many serious miscalculations, being far in excess of what they had been led to expect in comparison with their own.

It is interesting to compare the first bombing operation of the war to be carried out by Britain, who had never wanted war and was not prepared for it. As at Pearl Harbour, the targets were enemy battleships riding at anchor. These were units of the German High Seas Fleet at the western end of the Kiel Canal and in Schillig Roads off Wilhelmshaven. Young airmen who had of course never before operated against hostile forces were ordered to attack them in Blenheim, Wellington and Hampden twin-engined bombers. Guy Gibson, who was later to lead the famous Mohne Dam raid, flew one of the Hampdens and describes what happened in his book *Enemy Coast Ahead*.[1] It is almost startling to read that the recommended height for the attack (with armour-piercing bombs, not torpedoes) was 3,000 feet and that 'none of us had ever taken off

[1] Michael Joseph (1946).

with a bomb load on before and we did not even know whether our Hampdens would unstick with 2,000 pounds of bombs'.

Fortunately weather conditions were poor and only a small number of aircraft found the targets, causing some superficial damage to the cruiser *Emden* and the pocket battleship *Scheer*. Tragically enough, most of the bombs which hit their mark failed to explode; but seven aircraft were lost. The six from Gibson's squadron jettisoned their bombs without finding the target. 'So at last we landed. It was my first landing in a Hampden at night, and I think that went for all.'

By contrast it is fair to mention at this point the splendid night attack on Italian warships at Taranto by 22 Swordfish of the Fleet Air Arm, flying from the *Illustrious* a year later. Most of the Swordfish were armed with torpedoes but some carried bombs. Between them they sank or immobilised 3 out of 6 Battleships and, in the space of an hour, seriously crippled the Italian Navy. The Japanese are said to have shown the keenest interest in this operation in which many of the problems which were to face them at Pearl Harbour were similar – for instance the difficulties of keeping torpedoes on a shallow run in harbour conditions.

Only three days after Pearl Harbour, Britain suffered the shattering loss of the battleship *Prince of Wales,* one of her largest and most modern ships, and the battle-cruiser *Repulse* off Malaya with heavy loss of life. This was the first taste the British were to have of Japanese bombing and its unexpected accuracy. Unlike the Pearl Harbour attack and the operations off Ceylon which are to be described later on in this book, these ships were sunk by land-based Navy Air Force bombers, twin-engined machines of similar types to those used by the British in their first raid of 4th September 1939 against German warships. These were mainly Navy Type 96 twin-engined bombers, with a few newer Type 01.

Japanese planes, incidentally, were identified by their type and use, prefixed by the last two figures of the year in which they came into operational use according to the Japanese calendar. The year 1940 (Western style) was the year 2600 to the Japanese and the year 1936 was, to them, 2596. Thus the plane which was mainly responsible for the loss of the *Prince of Wales* and *Repulse* had come into operational use in 1936. The Zero fighter, first used in 1940, was in turn the Navy Type 00 (hence Zero) Carrier-borne fighter. For the sake of brevity the Americans later brought in code names – always Western style Christian names – which were soon in popular use by all the Allies. Hence the Navy Type 96 Attack Bomber was known as 'Nell', the Navy Type 97 4-engined Flying Boat was 'Mavis', the Navy Type 99 Dive-bomber was 'Val' and so on. The Zero was dubbed 'Zeke' but in fact this most successful fighter was always universally known as 'the Zero'.

At first sight, by comparison with the almost abortive attempt by British bombers at Schillig Roads, everything seems to have gone with smooth efficiency for the Japanese off Malaya on 10th December 1941. But a closer look makes it clear that, although expertly conceived and carried out things were far from straightforward for them. The whole force, consisting of 60 Nells and 24 Bettys (the newer Type 01), flew from bases in French Indo-China. They had all been astonished not to have been severely bombed the moment war broke out. Alas there were no long range bombers to do this and even medium range bombers from the RAF were not to appear to Japanese naval forces until four months later.

With Japanese troops landing in large numbers at Kota Bharu in Northern Malaya, the 26th Air Flotilla consisting of the Genzan, Kanoya and Mihoro Air Corps were standing by in the Saigon area to deal with any interference from the sea. Reconnaissance planes kept a careful watch on Singapore harbour where the *Prince of Wales* and *Repulse* were berthed. On the 9th photographs appeared to show them still there.

It was inconceivable that, with their enormous armament, they would not be sent north to pulverise the invasion fleet. A second Pearl Harbour was being hastily organised to deal with them at Singapore, when a Japanese submarine, *I–56*, sighted them well out to sea and heading northwards as expected. The Singapore photographs, it transpired, were of two large merchant ships, not of the warships at all. As darkness fell torpedo bombers were despatched and, after a long search, a heavy attack was about to be pressed home on a warship, lit by a large flare when, in the nick of time, she was identified as the *Chokai*, a heavy cruiser and the flag-ship of Vice-Admiral Jisaburo Ozawa. By this time the safety pins had been pulled on their torpedoes.

Each bomber had only the one and there were no spares, so in this dangerous condition they had to be flown back the considerable distance to their bases to be landed in the darkness. With very little sleep they were sent off again next day, 10th December, reconnaissance planes having gone ahead by an hour. It was 9.45 a.m. before the British ships were sighted, and 11 a.m. before the attack developed. By this time fuel supplies scarcely allowed the bombers a safe return.

After the previous night's error in identification the airmen were much worried that the battleship below them was the *Kongo,* which they thought it much resembled. With little time to spare messages such as 'Is not the fleet ours?' 'It looks like our *Kongo* to me,' were being exchanged.

But from this point on, once they were sure the ships were British, complete success was to be theirs. Vice-Admiral Sir Tom Phillips, C-in-C of the Far East Fleet, was in the *Prince of Wales* (Captain John Leach, RN). He had served at one time with Sir Arthur ('Bomber') Harris on the Joint Planning Staff of the Committee of Imperial Defence and they were old friends. Captain Leach, as it happens, had also been at the Army Staff College with Sir Arthur in 1928–1929. 'Both,' he recalls, 'treated air versus battleship with ribaldry.'

Both were lost with the *Prince of Wales.*

Air Vice-Marshal Harris (as he then was) was Deputy Chief of Air Staff when the Admiral left to take command of the Far East Fleet. His parting words had been prophetic:

'Tom, you've never believed in air. Never get out from under the air umbrella; if you do you'll be for it. And as you flutter up to heaven all you'll say is – "My gosh, some sailor laid a hell of a mine for me." ' [1]

The air umbrella available off Malaya was nothing but a flimsy parasol, but Vice-Admiral Phillips did not take his friend's advice. A few Buffalo fighters were available but he did not wish to break wireless silence; appalled at this omission, but too late to be of use, Captain Tennant of the *Repulse* signalled on his own responsibility. Fighters arrived only in time to see wreckage and survivors, as

[1] *Bomber Offensive*, Sir A. T. Harris – Collins (1947).

attendant destroyers and other small vessels picked them up.

The Japanese tactics were ingenious, though simple enough. Ever since the bomber aircraft had been evolved during World War I a great deal of thought had been given by air strategists to developing a reasonably accurate method of delivering bombs, particularly against a moving target, without subjecting the aircraft to enormous losses. Though fighter planes could disrupt attacks at any altitude it was not a difficult matter to fly above the truly effective range of anti-aircraft fire. But accuracy then became a great problem. A bomb which has been soundly designed aerodynamically does not drop vertically but carries on at the same speed as the aircraft dropping it. Even at the highest levels when (30 years ago) a plane might have travelled two to three miles between the moment of release of a bomb and its explosion on the ground, the bomb will only have dropped back a few hundred yards behind the aircraft. A moving target, such as a ship, has only to alter course a few degrees as the bombs are falling and she is safe. Of course she loses this immunity if a large number of bombers are attacking her at once, from different directions. Between the wars such a poor view had been taken of the accuracy of high level bombing that it is worth quoting Sir Arthur Harris again:

> I remember a one-time CIGS[1] giving us a lecture (at the Army Staff College) in the course of which, looking pointedly at me as the sole surviving airman on the course, he, to all intents and purposes, dared me to challenge his assertion that Gibraltar was so small that a bomber could not even hit the place; he then asked me what percentage of hits on Gibraltar I would consider reasonable. I replied 99%, allowing for a 1% hang-up on the bomb racks.

Dive-bombing was always likely to be more effective. Yet at the time of which we are speaking the British, alone amongst the leading air powers, had never developed a dive-bomber of any importance although 16 Blackburn Skuas of Nos. 800 and 803

[1] Field Marshal Lord Cavan.

Squadrons, Fleet Air Arm, were the first to sink a major warship by dive-bombing. This they did flying from the Orkneys at maximum range, destroying the German cruiser *Königsberg* in Bergen Fiord during the Norwegian operations in April and May 1940.

Attacking as the sun rose, they had the advantage of surprise. The cruiser had in fact suffered prior damage from the Norwegian shore batteries and was incapable of manoeuvre at the time of the attack. But the claim is valid enough. It is all the more surprising therefore that the three squadrons of Skuas, which is all the Fleet Air Arm had at that time, swiftly disappeared from the scene and were not replaced until two years later when that unattractive aircraft the Barracuda was brought into service with the Fleet Air Arm. By then it was realised that the importance and effectiveness of the dive-bomber had been sadly underestimated.

This aircraft was used with some success against the *Tirpitz*, immobilised in a Norwegian Fiord and against oil targets in Sumatra. Heavy losses suffered in June 1942 when Skuas attacked the *Scharnhorst* ineffectually at Trondheim may have had much to do with the decision to scrap the Skua. Certainly the slowness and vulnerability of the dive-bomber militated against its extended use. Such a plane had to be small, manoeuvrable and above all light in weight or the dive earthwards became too fast and unmanageable, even with the use of dive brakes. Fixed undercarriages seem to have been a regular feature contributing further to lightness and slowness. The dive-bomber in the absence of heavy fighter protection had little chance against hostile air attack and escorting fighters were hard put to it to protect dive-bombers, not only at the top of their dive but during their descent as well and also on recovery and reformation.

The German Junkers 87 or Stuka (an abbreviated form of Sturzkampflugzeug) had fantastic success in support of the infantry in Poland, France, Crete and Russia, pinpointing and eliminating, with an accuracy which the level bombers could never emulate, such targets as pillboxes and tanks.

Because Stuka losses were severe in the Battle of Britain and because the medium and heavy bombers were able to do much more damage against large urban targets in good visibility, the Stuka was dismissed by British air experts as comparatively ineffectual. This view has held to this day and certainly helped to foster the abandonment of the dive-bomber by the Fleet Air Arm (it had never been used in the Royal Air Force). But this does less than justice to the Stuka. Even in the Battle of Britain this aircraft was responsible for much accurate bombing of aerodromes. Its success in the absence of weighty air opposition in support of the Panzer Groups in Europe cannot be gainsaid. The Ju 87 was continued in use by the Luftwaffe as a front line bomber throughout 1940, 1941, 1942 and much of 1943. Furthermore it played a most successful part in early attacks on shipping in the English Channel as well as against British warships in the withdrawal from Crete and the Mediterranean convoys of 1942. For the latter operations quite a few were flown by Italians.

On the whole the Stuka more than paid its way for the Germans. Alan Moorehead in *The Desert War* (Hamish Hamilton) rightly says:

> It is useless for military strategists to argue, as they will and fiercely, that the Stuka is a failure and very vulnerable. Ask the troops in the field.

The Americans had shown themselves more alive to the value of the dive-bomber, particularly against shipping. Trials against old captured German warships had been conducted soon after World War I, but results were not clear-cut enough to prevent a plethora of opposing views. Like naval authorities the world over, the Americans tended to accept that the capital ship, suitably escorted and defended, had little to fear from the air. The Douglas Dauntless Dive-bomber was, however, in service in some numbers with the US Navy in 1941. This would prove itself in the Battles of the Coral Sea and Midway in May and June 1942, though losses were fearful.

As the war progressed and experience was gained in attacking ships at sea a different method altogether gained favour. If a ship's defences were poor enough or her gun crews taken sufficiently unawares this method was to fly in at mast height and to drop the bombs a few moments before reaching the target ship. These then entered the side of the vessel at great speed and bomb-aiming, once the knack was attained, had only to be a cursory business.

Admittedly against heavily armed ships without the element of surprise casualties from this type of low level attack were always fearfully high. Blenheims of No. 2 Bomber Group who tried the system in attacks on shipping in the English Channel were decimated.

The Japanese High Command had discovered for themselves how ineffective high-level bombing was bound to be against ships afloat on the high seas and had seriously considered abandoning the method. It was only because of the insistence of Admiral Yamamoto, Commander-in-Chief of the Imperial Combined Fleet, that high level bombing was not given up completely, and reliance placed exclusively on the two weapons with which they were to show, after intensive training, that they were past-masters; the dive-bomber – at this stage the Navy Type 99 (Val) with fixed undercarriage, carrying a crew of two and the Torpedo-bomber – the three seater Type 97 (Kate).

Against the *Prince of Wales* and *Repulse* the 26th Air Flotilla, which for once had to operate out of range of fighter protection, used an intelligent combination of high-level and torpedo-bombing.

High level bombers, at some 9,000 feet, appeared over the ships and attracted the attention of everyone. Anti-aircraft was loosed off and the din, confusion and smoke which resulted was all the Japanese required to distract attention from their low flying torpedo bombers, timed to arrive very shortly after the high level attack. The latter was fairly easily avoided by strong evasive action. The ships changed course violently and bombs, which had been released a full minute before, fell harmlessly where their targets might have been if a steady course had been held. The ships righted themselves and recovered. All on board heaved a sigh of relief as they watched the departing planes above them. At this moment torpedo-bombers flew in at sea level from a different direction and many had dropped their tin fish before their presence was realised. Although after their long search the Japanese attacks were only rather hastily co-ordinated, this well conceived plan was well carried out.

There was nothing amateur about the Japanese Air Forces. This much now had to be recognised.

And faced.

In contrast to the young men who took off from air-fields in Norfolk and Lincolnshire for their first raid of the war, with no prior experience of flying with a bomb load of one ton, let alone of dropping such a load, the Japanese had had the advantage of operational flying against limited Chinese opposition for over four years as well as of prolonged practical training against such targets as the old de-commissioned battleship *Settsu*, specially converted for the purpose. Though often accused of the slavish copying of the West, here was a sphere in which Japan had shown some originality. Although at the time of which we write the lesson had probably not yet sunk in, she had proved two things which few Allied naval strategists had been prepared to admit before. Indeed until Pearl Harbour most would have hotly denied their validity.

In spite of the comparatively poor results by both Allied and Axis flyers in Europe, accompanied often by severe losses, the enormous potentialities of the air weapon against warships had been proved to the hilt. This was the first point Japanese airmen had made. Secondly they had doomed to extinction, once and for all, the heavy battleship, of which none to-day exist throughout the navies of the world. It was a great shock to those who still believed that sea power depended on the battleship, and that the only answer to the battleship was another battleship, preferably with longer range and heavier armament. It was a boon in disguise, too, for governments whose finances were being stretched beyond endurance in the costly race to build bigger and better 'battle-waggons'. By the time World War II had ended and the score could be totted up, none had been worth their incredibly high cost. One after the other they made excellent targets for the torpedo or the aerial bomb and hardly any of them repaid in solid gain the trouble which lighter fleet units had to expend in protecting them. The *Hood*, the *Arizona*, the *Bismarck*, the *Cavour*, the *Roma*, the *Prince of Wales*, the *Tirpitz*, the *Oklahoma* – cosseted like outsize cuckoos in the nest, all finished on the bottom having helped their countries little and cost enormous loss of life. The Japs' own battleships went the same way. The *Yamato* (at 64,000 tons the biggest ever built) the *Haruna*, the *Musashi*, the *Ise*.

But they had not failed to grasp the lesson. Two of their front line aircraft-carriers, the *Kaga* and *Akagi*, were conversions; the first

from a battleship, the second from a battle cruiser. The *Shinano,*
which was on the stocks in 1942 had been intended as a battleship
but was completed as a carrier, though she was torpedoed and sunk
on her maiden voyage by an American submarine.

For it was the aircraft carriers which were to count in all
subsequent engagements.

The absence of all the American aircraft-carriers at Pearl
Harbour at the time of the raid was one of the few blessings to
emerge and the full weight of the attack fell on the very battleships
which this attack was proving obsolete. Subsequent naval battles
were fought without them and it is perfectly true to say that the
Americans would have been worse off if it had been otherwise.

Meanwhile it is worth looking at the score, taking Pearl Harbour
and the loss of the *Prince of Wales* and *Repulse* together. Apart from
the loss of minor vessels, of which there were many at Pearl
Harbour, the Japanese had put out of commission or sunk nine
battleships and killed 3,250 men in the space of 4 days. Her losses
were 32 planes, one submarine, 5 midget submarines and perhaps
200 men.

CHAPTER TWO

Matters Politic

'We cannot help the war effort of British Imperialism.'
PANDIT JAWAHARLAL NEHRU.

Churchill's concern at Japanese successes sprang as much from the political developments of the period as from the military and naval situation. These had little publicity at the time, and few of the sailors and airmen who were involved in the struggle can have had any inkling of what was going on in this field.

Sir Stafford Cripps, until then British Ambassador in Moscow, but recently appointed Lord Privy Seal and, as such, a member of the British War-time Coalition Government, arrived in New Delhi on 23rd March 1942. Cripps's unenviable task was to bring India into line as an ally and partner in the war against Japan. For by now the Eastern borders of Assam and Bengal had suddenly become the front line of the battle, a conception which would have seemed inconceivable only four months before. It was scarcely a propitious moment.

Nehru and other Indian leaders had only recently been freed from gaol for allegedly inflammatory speeches, made at the end of 1940. The exact date of their release – 3rd December 1941 – preceded the outbreak of the war in Asia by four days. Was this by luck or by good judgment? For British motives might have been suspect if the releases had followed and not preceded Pearl Harbour.

The 'inflammatory speeches' had been part of the campaign formulated by the Indian National Congress of *satyagraha* (literally 'adherence to truth' but to become a connotation for the practice of non-violent resistance to British rule in India). Approximately 6,000 were imprisoned for varying terms in 1940 and 1941 for adherence to or encouragement of this policy.

Not unnaturally, with British hands tied by the war in Europe, the opportunity to cut adrift from British rule had seemed to Indian leaders to have taken on an inviting brightness. In this they felt they had the support of the United States of America, as indeed Roosevelt made it clear they had. But even with Britain's hands tied, India's 390 million population, poverty-stricken, mute, tradition-bound, caste-ridden and disunited by religion, politics, race, language and social distinction, could be harnessed to no greater threat to British rule than to non-co-operation; a comfortably negative policy which came easily to the Asiatic as active resistance would never have done. If one sat and did nothing one could be said to be non-co-operative, or passively resisting the Government of India which was in effect the Indian Civil Service for early on in the War the Congress ministries in the provinces had resigned.

Once the war had spread to the East, India's leaders were faced with a different situation altogether. What they needed above all was to be left in peace, to their own devices. What they were now to be faced with was the choice between continued dependence on Britain or annexation, perhaps conquest by, or at least subservience to, Japan.

India's leaders strove lamely for independence still, blinding themselves to the realities of the situation. If they stuck their heads in the sand, they felt, perhaps the Imperialists from the West, and equally those from the East, would go away.

Gandhi told the British: 'Don't leave India to Japan, but leave India to Indians in an orderly manner.'

It just could not be done, of course, with things as they were in 1942. The British were to do just this when the war was over. Or, at least, they were to do their best to. The disorder and bloodshed that followed was always predictable, but could not be laid at Britain's door. One thing is certain: the massive disturbances with which Independence was accompanied in 1948 could never have been tolerated in 1942.

To the combatants in World War II India was a bone of contention which could not conceivably be abandoned. From a global point of view her importance might become incalculable.

If the German offensive against Russia, which in March 1942, six months before Stalingrad, seemed to be sweeping all before it, were to continue unchecked, the invaluable Middle East oil supplies, vital to the West, would be imperilled. An India friendly to Japan, or even an India passively non-co-operating, could close the gap between Japan and Germany by over 2000 miles. China, too, would have been cut off completely from all effective help. German and Italian armies were firmly lodged on Egypt's frontiers and until El Alamein in November the Axis threat from that direction, with the prospect to the Allies of the loss of the Suez Canal, seemed even more pressing than the threat through the Caucasus.

It is true that this broad strategic view did not take into account the enormous difficulties over communications which would have arisen. Only the flimsiest of tracks connected Burma with India, and Afghanistan had scarcely any road or rail communications. Yet sea and air routes would have been open to the Japanese.

How could India be left to its own devices at such a moment? Britain had felt as early as 1940 that India's wholehearted support for the War was essential. It had even been thought possible that the Japanese, by then heavily involved in Indo-China as well as with China, might hesitate to enter the war on a broader basis, if convinced that India was firmly against her. Britain could not foresee that within eighteen months it was to become a matter of life or death to the Allies.

It is true that Indian leaders and the comparatively small proportion of its teeming masses who knew or cared about such things, recognising that the devil you know is better than the devil you don't, offered co-operation with the British against Japan. But only in return for complete autonomy. Nehru several times made it clear that *satyagraha* was essentially a policy for civilians and was not intended to be followed by the many thousands of Indians in the armed services, whose loyalty in the end proved magnificent. Many serving soldiers, such as Sikhs and Muslims, would never, in any event have wished to serve under a government in which the Indian National Congress formed the predominant element. In Asia to this day the first loyalties of the people are to their religion and their community.

But India had to put to advantage the enormous bargaining power suddenly thrust into her hands by Japan's entry into the war and could not let it fall from her grasp. Yet so long as her distaste for Japanese suzerainty was felt and expressed, as it inevitably was, this bargaining power lost much of its strength.

Before the spread of the war to Asia, Nehru, whose attitude towards Britain during the war was far more understanding and conciliatory than Gandhi's, had expressed India's views in the following terms:

'We have made it perfectly clear in the past that we cannot help the war effort of British imperialism or become its recruiting sergeants.

'We adhere to our policy of non-violence in our struggle for freedom in all its implications.'

Once Japan had entered the fray the British Government had hoped for a more positive outlook, but did not really find it. Nehru summed up the modified Indian outlook thus:

'The United Nations should acknowledge the independence of India. Meanwhile we are urging the people to oppose the aggressor and on no account to submit to the invader. But individual resistance is of little avail.

'I do feel definitely that it would be a tragedy for the world if Germany and Japan won this war and dominated the world. I do not want this to happen.

'I am not going to give in to Britain if she wants to exploit or rule India. Much less do I want the Indian people to give in or be passive towards the Japanese. I want to resist them to the uttermost.

'Our policy concerning the Japanese invasion is that we are out to embarrass Japan to the utmost.'

All these utterances of Pandit Jawarhal Nehru were made at the time and show how equivocal was India's policy towards the war.

Sir Stafford Cripps was deputed to see India's leaders and to offer them assurances of autonomy when peace returned 'within the Commonwealth', that half-way house between colonial domination and complete independence by which, in the event, the many units of the British Commonwealth were ultimately to sever the threads which had for so long bound them to the British Crown. Winston Churchill's implacable opposition to Indian constitutional reform had been a matter of common knowledge, but under compelling pressure he could no longer afford to hold to these views. Britain was already pledged to ultimate Dominion status, but beyond this Churchill could not go, and, imperialist as he was, he could not visualise the day when the rule of the British Raj in India would come to an end. 'I have not become the King's First Minister,' he was to proclaim, 'in order to preside over the dissolution of the British Empire.'

In the summer of 1940 the Congress Working Committee had made definite demands for complete independence and the establishment of a provisional National Government immediately, announcing its readiness to co-operate in the war effort in return. Many elements in Congress were opposed to offering such co-operation, but were persuaded of its necessity. Britain then expanded Indian representation on the Executive Council and made other conciliatory gestures. None of these were acceptable to Congress. The Viceroy, Lord Linlithgow, communicated to Congress in August 1940 a long statement from His Majesty's Government re-iterating Britain's intention that Dominion status was her objective in India, but making it clear that minority interests, particularly the Muslims, had the right to be considered and postponing action until after the cessation of hostilities.

The problem was indeed far less simple than it seemed at first sight. Millions, especially non-Hindus, would feel betrayed if summarily handed over to a predominantly Hindu government, and many of the Princes might have felt the same. This, of course, was not good enough for Congress. In the event *satyagraha* was pursued, and Indian leaders, as we have seen, were incarcerated. It was hardly a satisfactory situation as the Japanese approached.

Sir Stafford Cripps' offer, although presented in the guise of a new, more conciliatory one, was seen at once by the Indian leaders as a mere repetition of the pledge made by Lord Linlithgow in 1940. The Indian National Congress turned down the Cripps proposals as being vague and indeterminate, dependant on cessation of hostilities before having any practical effect. The Muslim League under Jinnah also found the offer unacceptable, but felt gratified that the possibility of a seceding Pakistan was impliedly recognised. The Hindu Mahasabha feared that the proposals as being vague and indeterminate, dependent on of opinion in the Native States.

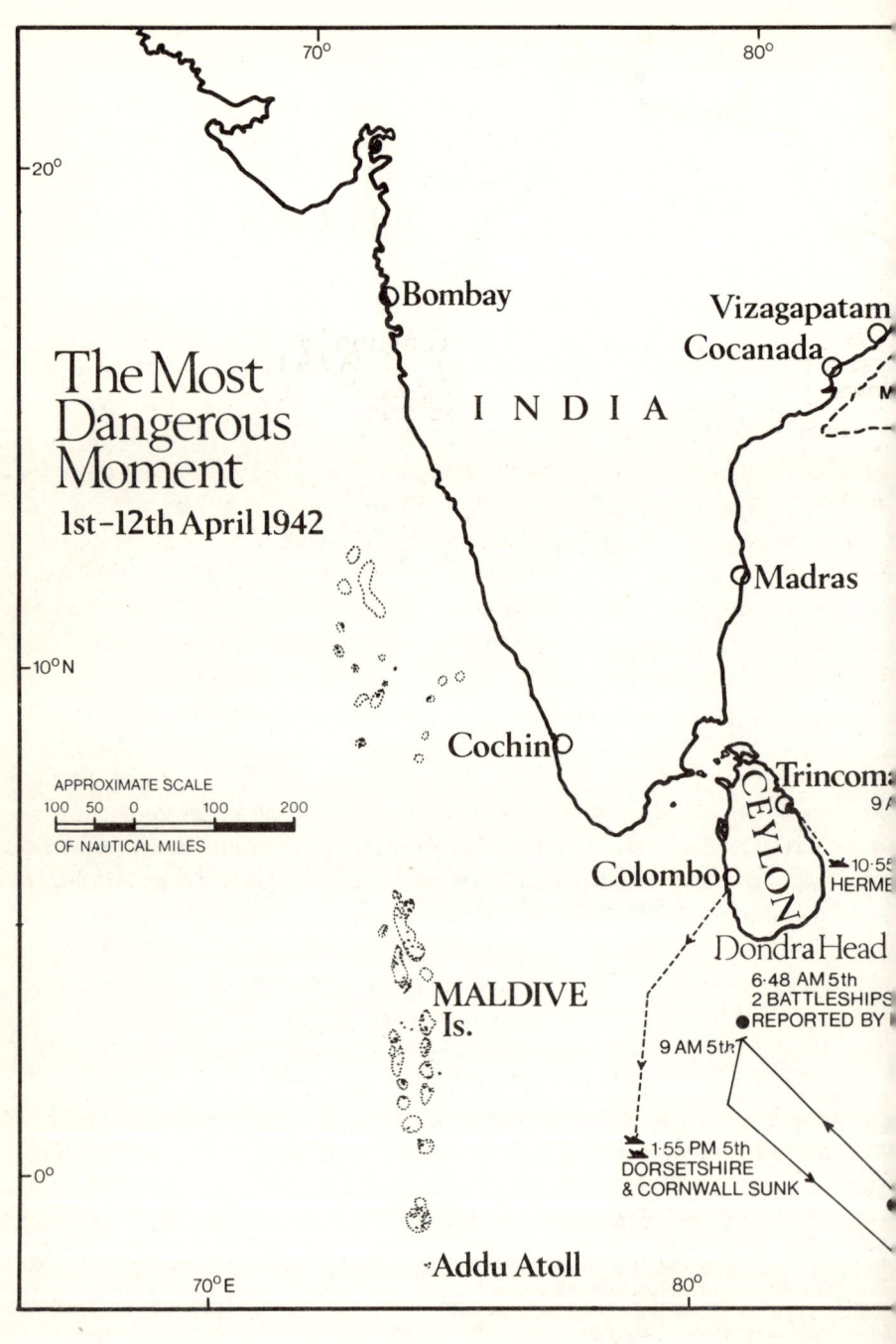

The Most
Dangerous
Moment
1st–12th April 1942

INDIA

Bombay

Vizagapatam
Cocanada

Madras

Cochin

Trincoma
9 A

CEYLON

Colombo

10·55
HERME

APPROXIMATE SCALE

100 50 0   100   200

OF NAUTICAL MILES

Dondra Head
6·48 AM 5th
2 BATTLESHIPS
REPORTED BY

MALDIVE
Is.

9 AM 5th

1·55 PM 5th
DORSETSHIRE
& CORNWALL SUNK

Addu Atoll

70°
80°

20°

10° N

0°

70° E
80°

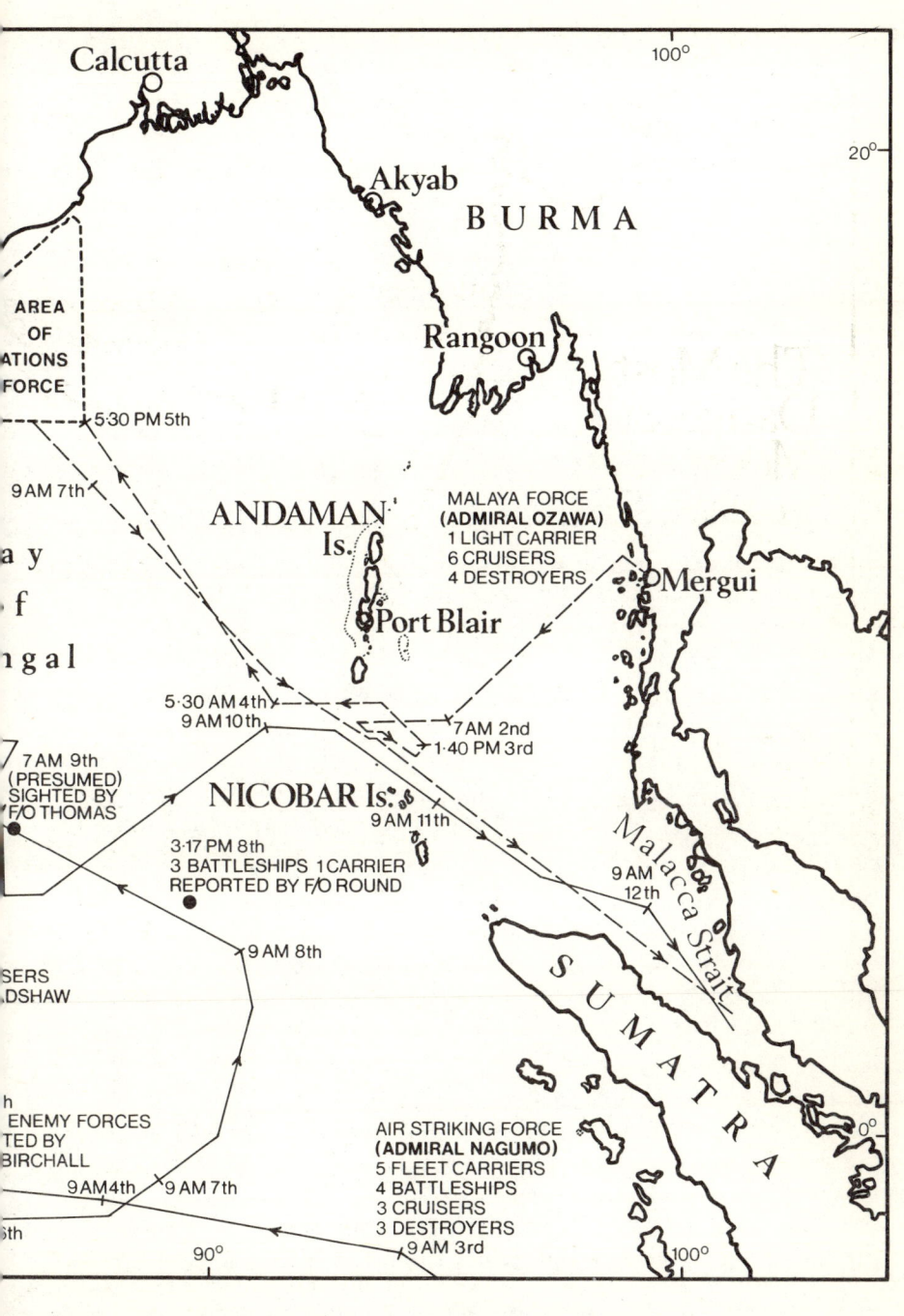

Calcutta

100°

20°

Akyab

B U R M A

Rangoon

AREA
OF
ATIONS
FORCE

5·30 PM 5th

9 AM 7th

ANDAMAN
Is.

MALAYA FORCE
(ADMIRAL OZAWA)
1 LIGHT CARRIER
6 CRUISERS
4 DESTROYERS

Mergui

a y

Port Blair

o f

5·30 AM 4th
9 AM 10th

7 AM 2nd
1·40 PM 3rd

n g a l

7 AM 9th
(PRESUMED)
SIGHTED BY
F/O THOMAS

NICOBAR Is.

9 AM 11th

3·17 PM 8th
3 BATTLESHIPS 1 CARRIER
REPORTED BY F/O ROUND

9 AM
12th

Malacca Strait

9 AM 8th

SERS
DSHAW

S U M A T R A

0°

h
ENEMY FORCES
TED BY
BIRCHALL

AIR STRIKING FORCE
(ADMIRAL NAGUMO)
5 FLEET CARRIERS
4 BATTLESHIPS
3 CRUISERS
3 DESTROYERS

9 AM4th

9 AM 7th

100°

5th

90°

9 AM 3rd

Satisfactory constitutional reform for India was obviously so complicated and difficult of attainment that it could scarcely be arranged in a few weeks. Even thirty years later the problems have not resolved themselves. After partition the massacre of half a million and communal rivalry, ancient and unbridgeable, caused only further disruption and misery. East Pakistan, as Bangla Desh, has seceded from West after bitter fighting and the fate of Kashmir still hangs in the air. It is hardly surprising therefore that the Cripps mission failed.

Elementary strategy made it clear that if Japan were to include India in her expansionist plans, Ceylon would prove a useful stepping stone. The combination of a land drive from Burma and a sea-borne invasion through Ceylon would have been a most effective way of subduing India. The Japanese certainly had the necessary naval power.

Politically, Ceylon, separated from her huge northern neighbour only by the narrow, shoal-bound Palk Strait, presented nothing like the problems of India. True, her inhabitants were far from being homogeneous, the majority Singhalese, of Aryan stock (would Hitler have accepted them as such?) being Buddhist, and the largest minority race being Tamil Hindus, of Dravidian stock. There were other minorities, but these were of small significance. All, in fact, including the earliest aboriginal Veddhas, had hailed from India; but Ceylon, being comparatively speaking a land of plenty and less populated than India, had bred peoples of a more easy-going nature than those who inhabited the huge continent to the north.

Scheduled to become, when the conflict was over, one of the first non-white countries in the British Colonial Empire to become independent, the transition was to be made with exemplary smoothness. Brought automatically into the War in 1939, the leaders of the country, unlike those of India, gave unstinting and ungrudging support to the cause of Britain and her Allies, and the two ports of Colombo on the West coast and Trincomalee to the north-east became even more important as links between Europe and the Far East than in peace time. With the loss of Malaya and the East Indies, Ceylon became of vast importance as a rubber producer. She agreed to 'slaughter tapping', which would shorten the life of the trees, and was given compensation in due course. Her entire tea production, too, went by contract to the British Board of Trade. For tea was a war weapon in itself. How could Britons have carried on through the trials and tribulations of the six year struggle without their 'cuppa'?

Ceylonese members of the State Council – and they predominate, although not having full responsible governmental powers – did not cease in their efforts towards full autonomy, but would always have been satisfied with Dominion Status. True, there were the younger hot-heads, particularly those with Marxist leanings, who raised their voices against 'foreign colonialism' and 'the Capitalist Oppressors', but their following was small. The various doctrinal differences, highlighted when Russia became an ally of Britain, were to keep Leftist elements in Ceylon in a continual state of antagonism towards each other right up until 1970 when most were united, without noticeable friction, in Mrs. Bandaranaike's coalition government. The lady in question, though by birth and up-bringing ultra-conservative, was at that time only mildly socialist; she was later to move ever leftwards in search of popular support.

Four of the more vociferous rebels found themselves put under detention, three of them fated to be given Ministries by Mrs. Bandaranaike a full 30 years later.

Under the wartime emergency legislation, the Governor, Sir Andrew Caldecott, had issued detention orders in June 1940 against five State Councillors, all members of the Lanka Sama Samaja (Ceylon Egalitarian, i.e Socialist) Party. These were Phillip Gunewardena, Dr N. M. Perera, Dr Colvin de Silva, Leslie Goonewardena and Edmund Samarakoddy. Only the latter two were not to reach Ministerial rank in due course, though Samarakoddy has led a large white-collar trade union for many years. Leslie Goonewardena, Secretary of the LSSP, managed to evade arrest and in due course secretly crossed to India. The other four were detained at the old military prison in Kandy, in the central foot-hills of the Island and at one time the Capital. As in India the detainees were not charged with any offence, nor granted a trial, but at the expense of their liberty reasonable amicability prevailed throughout the country.

British troops, then, whether stationed in Ceylon or passing through to other theatres of war had mainly the pleasantest of memories of Lanka[1] (the Island) and generally speaking the Ceylonese reciprocated.

[1] Now officially the Republic of Sri (respected or blessed) Lanka. (See Preface).

CHAPTER THREE

The Allies Fall Back

'The combined fleet of the Allies was sunk in the forlorn
battle of the Java Sea.'
WINSTON CHURCHILL.

After Pearl Harbour and the loss of the *Prince of Wales* and *Repulse*,
Hong Kong and Singapore had soon surrendered and the Allies'
naval strength in the Far East was reduced to a dangerous and
crippling level. Yet Japan had suffered no significant losses and her
offensive continued unabated further south and west. A naval force
had perforce to be scraped together as a combined fleet to do what
it could to stem the flood. Known as the Eastern Striking Force,
this was assembled at Soerabaya, in Java, at the end of February.

No battleships or aircraft carriers were available. The Force was
composed only of cruisers and destroyers, and four nations pooled
their resources to make up the fleet. This consisted of the Cruisers
De Ruyter (flagship) and *Java* (Dutch), *Exeter* (British), *Houston*
(American) and *Perth* (Australian). The destroyers were the *Electra*,
Encounter and *Jupiter* (British), *Kortenaer* and *Witte de With* (Dutch),
and *John D. Edwards*, *Alden*, *John D. Ford* and *Paul Jones* (American).
Other vessels, the Dutch cruiser *Tromp*, the Australian cruiser
Hobart, the British light cruisers *Danae* and *Dragon*, the Dutch
destroyers *Evertsen*, *van Ghent* and *Banckert*, the American destroyers
Edsall, *Stewart*, *Parrott* and *Pillsbury*, the British destroyers *Scout* and
Tenedos and the American aircraft tender *Langley*, though not part of
the Far Eastern Striking Force, were also involved in the ensuing or
slightly earlier operations in the Java Sea area.

The command of the combined fleet had been given to the Dutch
Rear-Admiral Karel W. F. M. Doorman and its task was to hold
up, even if it could not prevent, Japanese occupation of the Dutch
East Indies. The Force laboured under many disadvantages. It had
no capital ships and no air cover. There were difficulties of
communication and there had been no opportunity to operate

together as a cohesive force. Yet they bravely put to sea and, in operations extending over the afternoon and night of 27th February, were almost wiped out by superior Japanese forces, for whom it was a classic example of the offensive use of sea power. The Japanese had the enormous advantage of numerous supporting aircraft, both by day and by night. Their air spotting in the dark was very efficient and by dropping flares they were able to indicate every change of course so that the Allied ships found evasion impossible.

Churchill described the Battle of the Java Seas in the telling phrase 'this forlorn battle'. It was certainly a humiliating defeat, both in its speed and its completeness. When the engagement was over the last remnants of the Allied fleet, the *Hobart* and most of the American destroyers, limped southwards to Australia. The only Dutch vessel to survive the catastrophe, the *Tromp,* together with the *Danae, Dragon, Scout* and *Tenedos* managed to reach Ceylon. Casualties were very heavy indeed and included the Dutch Admiral. Survivors, whose trials had scarcely begun were cast up on the various islands in the vicinity.

The Indian Ocean now lay open and undefended.

How soon could Japan take advantage of the strategic situation? She first had enormous territories to occupy and consolidate. No one in history had conquered so much in such a short time. It cannot even be said that she needed to pause and lick her wounds. For such as she had endured had been superficial.

Japan was infinitely more interested in Eastern Asia than in the Pacific. Though her motives had always been couched in the most benign terms, as expansionism so often is, her eyes were directed towards Asia and not Eastwards into the Pacific. But the latter was the theatre of war in which America had first to be eliminated before Japan could give her full attention to her sublime mission of liberating those in bondage and incorporating them under her tutelage in the Greater East Asia Co-Prosperity Sphere, conceived almost ten years before, when Manchuria became the first unwilling conscript.

Americans still held out in the Philippines, and were to do so, with great heroism and fortitude, until mid-May. Australians would stoutly defend New Guinea. Malaya had gone. It was now

Burma's turn and for most of March British attention was focussed here.

Japan was surprisingly confident at this stage that America could be eliminated as a force that counted in the Western Pacific. She was equally sure that Germany would succeed in the Middle East and Russia and would cut off Britain from American help. Her military and naval forces therefore continued to press forward on every front.

Though Churchill could not have known it, Admiral Raeder, the German Naval C-in-C, in a report to Hitler dated 13th February 1942, wrote:

> Japan plans to protect this front in the Indian Ocean by capturing the key position of Ceylon, and she also plans to gain control of the sea in that area by means of superior naval forces. 15 Japanese submarines are at the moment operating in the Bay of Bengal, in the waters off Ceylon and in the straits on both sides of Sumatra and Java . . .
>
> Once Japanese battleships, aircraft carriers and submarines and the Japanese Air Force are based on Ceylon, Britain will be forced to resort to heavily escorted convoys if she desires to maintain communications with India and the Near East.

Plans to strike westwards into the Indian Ocean and seize Ceylon had been prepared by the Staff of the Japanese Combined Fleet. They had gone further and had even envisaged taking over Madagascar, then in Vichy French hands, as they had virtually taken over Indo-China.

Since Pearl Harbour there had been various meetings between Vice-Admiral Nomura, Japanese Naval Attaché in Berlin, and Admiral Fricke, Raeder's Chief of Staff, who did what he could to persuade the Japanese to initiate operations which would assist and support Germany's own efforts against Britain. Clearly the sphere in which such co-operation was most feasible was the western Indian Ocean, in the direction of the Red Sea and Persian Gulf; the seizure of Ceylon and Madagascar would be an excellent preliminary step.

The OKM (*Oberkommando der Marine*) wasted no time. On 21st

February the German Naval Attaché in Tokyo was providing the
Japanese with particulars of suitable landing places in Ceylon and
Fricke, conferring with Nomura again on the 27th March,
expressed a lively desire that the Japanese should begin operations
against the sea routes in the northern Indian Ocean. Just such an
operation had in fact been put in train the day before, though it is
most unlikely that Nomura knew this.

The Andaman and Nicobar Islands, the former an Indian penal
colony and both undefended, were occupied by the Japanese on
23rd March, but this was the last occupation westwards that they
were to undertake. At this stage their attention, as they were
perfectly well aware, must be directed into the Pacific.

No time was wasted in basing a detachment of 13 Long range
flying-boats at Port Blair in the Andamans and the Japanese now
felt assured that they could safely reinforce their troops in Burma
by sea to Rangoon, which the British had evacuated on 9th March.
The flying-boats' long range patrols proved of great value during
the ensuing fortnight.

With the threat to Ceylon clearly developing, it is worth
reviewing the succession of calamities, with which Winston
Churchill had been confronted during February and March 1942.

The situation in the Middle East was one of his prime concerns.
This was the only theatre in which British land forces were in touch
with the Germans and Italians.

At the end of January Rommel was advancing on Egypt and
people were already shouting his name in the streets of Cairo.
Egyptians were not necessarily pro-Axis or anti-British in feeling,
but took the natural view that if the Axis were to win the War, as
seemed to many a distinct possibility at the time, they should show
themselves in sympathy with the victors. Sir Miles Lampson, the
British Ambassador (later Lord Killearn), had every reason to
believe that King Farouk, who had just been faced with the
resignation of his government, was about to appoint a new pro-Axis
regime. On the night of 4th February he boldly forced his way into
the Abdin Palace and, after threatening to compel Farouk's
abdication, succeeding in obtaining his approval of a pro-British
government under Nahas Pasha, who was to stay in power almost
to the end of the war. Though scarcely in accord with the best

principles of democracy, Sir Miles Lampson's bold move was of enormous importance to Britain and was perhaps in the end of more benefit to Egypt than would have been a capitulation to Germany and Italy.

Churchill had become more and more impatient with General Sir Claude Auchinleck and was in favour of replacing him if he could not launch an immediate counter-offensive against Rommel. Lord Alanbrooke (then General Sir Alan Brooke), Chief of the Imperial General Staff, had the greatest difficulty, as he has subsequently told us, in urging patience on the Prime Minister. Auchinleck was summoned to London early in March but felt he could not leave Cairo at such a moment. In the event Sir Alan Brooke's Vice-Chief, Lieutenant-General Sir Archibald Nye, as we will see later on in this story, was sent out to put the Prime Minister's views to him and to obtain a full report on his plans from Auchinleck. It did not, in the end, save 'The Auk' from the loss of the command of the Middle East forces.

Within a week of the situation in Cairo being retrieved by Sir Miles Lampson, the two German battle-cruisers *Scharnhorst* and *Gneisenau*, which had been bottled up at Brest for six months with Bomber Command devoting much of its energies to their destruction, with only modest success, but at the expense of heavy losses, ran the gauntlet up the English Channel back to Germany. The voyage was made safer than it might have been by heavy low cloud, for which the Germans had carefully waited.

Though essentially a naval matter, there were no heavy units of the Royal Navy available to challenge the two cruisers. Except in the farthest north and west, no warships had been hazarded in Home waters since the earliest days of hostilities. So it fell to the lot of the Fleet Air Arm to dispute their passage up the Channel and, since they were few in number and with great gallantry endured enormous losses, Bomber Command, trained for quite different work, had to be called in.

As it happens the Command was in process of changing Commanders-in-Chief. Sir Arthur Harris had not yet taken over and Air Marshal Sir Richard Peirse had left for Java and would command air forces in South-East-Asia for the rest of the war. It would be interesting to know his feelings on learning of the battle-cruisers' escape for he had been taxed with failure to destroy the *Scharnhorst* and *Gneisenau* at Brest and this must have been one of the factors which cost him the command. Yet he had never hesitated to order an enormous number of sorties against the German warships and bomber crews had tried manfully to put them out of commission. The writer served throughout the operative period with a Hampden Squadron (No. 106) which took part in many of the attacks, including an unusual daylight attack in June 1941. This somewhat desperate measure was occasioned by the unexpected movement of one of the cruisers southward to La Pallice. In common with many others this squadron lost many crews over Brest, including that of a CO, Wing Commander Polglase, who had volunteered to go in low to be sure of hits.

Now as the *Scharnhorst* and *Gneisenau,* with attendant minesweepers under a formidable air umbrella, made their dash through the Channel, flyers from both the Fleet Air Arm and the Royal Air Force, with low cloud and poor visibility to hinder them, tried manfully to get at the battle-cruisers. Suffering heavy casualties in the process, they did what they could to sink such inviting targets presented to them on their very doorstep. They did manage to damage both ships by laying mines in their projected eastward course.

When the two ships got through it was a great shock to the nation. Not unnaturally comparisons were made with the Japanese successes against warships which we have been considering. The German ships, however, had the advantage of very heavy air protection for the whole journey and this made all the difference. As it happens, neither the *Scharnhorst* nor *Gneisenau* were to take any further effective part in the war, but there was every reason to dread their possible use against merchant shipping in the Atlantic. Sorties of this kind had brought enormous successes for the Germans in the early part of the war.

Four days later, on 15th February, Singapore fell. 'The greatest disaster to British arms which our history affords,' Churchill was to call it.

At about the same time an entire convoy, which Admiral Sir Andrew Cunningham was trying to run from Alexandria to beleaguered Malta, where oil supplies were running dry, succumbed to air and sea attacks. Every ship in the convoy was sunk. February closed with 'the forlorn battle' of the Java Seas and the abandonment of the Dutch East Indies.

On 9th March the invasion of New Guinea began and in Burma Rangoon was lost. By the end of the month the realisation was accepted that British and Indian troops in Burma, as well as the Chinese force under the American General Stilwell, could no longer contain the Japanese advance, nor even seriously delay it. The problem now, as it had been at Dunkirk, was to extricate as many of the troops as possible. The difficulties far exceeded those at Dunkirk, however; the distances were incomparably greater and the outside assistance that could be given was virtually nil. There was no real road communication with India and, since the valleys up which retreating troops were forced to move, ran mainly to the north and north-east, nothing could be done to help them by sea. To leave Burma one had to walk. And walk the survivors did, many civilian refugees dying of cholera en route or from starvation and thirst.

U-Boat sinkings for the month of March rose to three quarters of a million tons.

Lastly Sir Stafford Cripps was already envisaging the failure of his mission to enlist Indian co-operation.

Although Churchill was now sustained by the one great consoling factor that the might of the United States of America had been thrown into the War on our side, even to his indomitable spirit this was a mournful catalogue of events. Another calamity on the same scale might bring down the Coalition Government and compel Britain to throw in her hand.

And so the most dangerous and distressing moment of the War for Mr Churchill had arrived.

The Japanese Naval High Command did not pause long before turning their attention westwards into the Indian Ocean. A large fleet, under Vice-Admiral Chuichi Nagumo, substantially the same force which he had led against Pearl Harbour in the opening attack of the War, left Kendari in the Celebes on 26th March. Steering southwards, they entered the Indian Ocean via the Ombai Straits, between Flores and Timor.

A smaller fleet, known as the 'Malaya Force', left Mergui, the small Burmese port on the Kra Isthmus, from which it had been recently operating to cover Japanese occupation of the Andamans and Nicobar Islands. Sailing a few days later in order to synchronise their entry into the Indian Ocean with Nagumo's First Air Fleet, this Force was commanded by Vice-Admiral Jisaburo Ozawa, who had come so near to being torpedoed by his own planes the evening before the *Prince of Wales* and *Repulse* had been lost.

Nagumo would be operating at extended range. He therefore refuelled his ships from oilers at sea and pressed on westwards.

CHAPTER FOUR

Ceylon Prepares

'My old battle boats are in various states of disrepair.'
ADMIRAL SIR JAMES SOMERVILLE,
of the British Eastern Fleet.

We now know that, even before Pearl Harbour, the Americans had managed to crack the Japanese wireless code in which all top secret diplomatic messages were exchanged between Tokyo and their embassies abroad. It is clearly from this invaluable source that we were now presented with the most accurate foreknowledge of Japanese intentions. On the very morning that Nagumo and his Fleet sailed from Kendari (26th March), Admiral Sir James Somerville, the newly appointed C-in-C Eastern Fleet, who had only arrived in the Island on the 24th, was warning his Captains at a conference in Colombo that a Japanese attack could be expected. He even ventured to forecast 31st March for the attack.

Captain Augustus Agar, VC, one of his Captains and no stranger to Ceylon, where his father had been a tea planter and he himself had been born, writes in his autobiography, *Footprints in the Sea:* [1]

> There was an airman present at this conference whose name I cannot recall [He was Air Vice-Marshal d'Albiac, Air Officer Commanding No 222 Group in Ceylon] but I remember most clearly his forceful exposition of the Japanese plan of attack as he visualised it. He reckoned it would be directed towards Ceylon and the Bay of Bengal in a three-pronged thrust, and he proved right in every detail. We were all most impressed, including the Admiral, who profited tremendously from the opinion and also the advice this airman gave. He said he expected these attacks . . . to be directed to Colombo and Trincomalee and one up the Bay of Bengal on our shipping, in separate strikes, which is exactly what took place . . .
> Evans Bros. Ltd.

So for once, it seemed, there was to be no element of surprise so far as the Services were concerned. Few of Ceylon's civilian population, though, had any inkling that this peaceful island was to shine briefly in the forefront of the battle. The war had so far touched them very little. Many of the young Europeans had 'gone off to the War' and would most of them see service with Indian Army Units from Burma to North Africa. Their women and children, too, had only recently left at the authorities' suggestion. South Africa received many of them.

When Singapore had fallen on 15th February, Admiral Sir Geoffrey Layton, who had been superseded by and then succeeded the luckless Admiral Sir Tom Phillips as C-in-C Far Eastern Fleet, finding himself with no Headquarters and no fleet to command, finished up in Ceylon.

In London the Chiefs of Staff Committee had just come to the wise and momentous decision that in every theatre of war there must be unified command, from whom the three Services must take their orders, and not from their respective Service Departments in London. This was a policy which was to be followed for the rest of the War on every front. Lord Alanbrooke has reported 'heated argument' over the point, but there can be no doubt of its wisdom.

Layton was therefore appointed C-in-C Ceylon, with powers which exceeded even those of the civilian Governor, Sir Andrew Caldecott. Using these extensive powers, and with the able assistance of Sir Oliver Goonetilleke (later Ceylon's first Ceylonese Governor-General) as Civil Defence Commissioner, he got straight down to business, organising the Island with vigour and speed for the trials ahead.

One of his first actions was to have an airstrip prepared across the Colombo Racecourse. Several houses, including the Chief Justice's, were in the projected flight path; so down they had to come. In these climes the monsoon winds, most conveniently for the aeronaut, blow for half the year from the south-west, and for the other half from the north-east. And the wind is mild on the odd occasions when this does not apply. This makes only a single runway necessary, instead of the usual three, in triangular fashion, which have to be laid out at airports elsewhere and for which room could never have been found at the Racecourse.

With everything to the East a lost cause, reinforcements had to come from the West. Fortunately they were coming in at a great pace.

As soon as the war spread to the Far East in December, large troop convoys were sent off on the long voyage to Singapore, via the Cape. Unhappily one arrived just before the city fell and units had no time to find their feet before they were over-run. Many of the new arrivals finished up in POW camps. One convoy had arrived in March, its forces being dispersed to India and Burma. Another, designated WS 16 (WS's were 'Winston's Specials') and consisting of 26 ships, taking between 40 and 50 thousand troops and much equipment to the Far East and North Africa, had assembled at Greenock, scheduled to sail in mid-February.

The Admiralty, with much prescience, had been alive to the probability that the battle-cruisers *Scharnhorst* and *Gneisenau* might soon slip out of Brest. They were concerned lest they might move westwards into the Atlantic. The safety of WS 16 was of such importance that they accordingly brought back most of Force H from the Mediterranean to Home Waters for its protection. For the British position in the East and even perhaps the results of El Alamein might well have depended on the convoy getting safely through.

Sir James Somerville, newly appointed to the command of the Eastern Fleet, had only recently handed over Force H to Vice-Admiral E. N. Syfret. He was now to set out eastwards with this convoy. It thus happened that when the convoy slipped out of the Firth of Clyde at midnight on 16th February, Admiral Somerville sailed in familiar company. They steamed out into a stormy North Atlantic, clear of the Irish coast. Included amongst the escorting warships was the battleship *Malaya,* fresh from repairs at New York after sustaining damage at Crete, the cruiser *Newcastle* and the carriers *Formidable* and *Eagle*.

It was in the *Formidable* that Admiral Somerville sailed. In less pretentious style the author, bound for the same theatre, was in a troopship called the *Empire Pride,* which I have always thought to have been somewhat of a misnomer. But I am pleased to see that she survived the war and was still trooping during the war in Korea. The *Eagle* had on board the first Spitfires to be flown in for

Malta's defence. In six months' time she was to end her days to a U-boat's torpedoes in the struggle to re-inforce Malta. The *Formidable* also was returning to service after a refit in the United States after running aground in the West Indies. She had taken on some American-built Martlet fighters in addition to her complement of Albacore bi-planes. The latter were a later version of the Swordfish, having much the same performance, but an enclosed cockpit.

Most of the convoy's escort were detached at Gibraltar and, because of the exigencies of the situation, *Formidable* went on ahead, arriving a fortnight before the troopships. To shorten the journey still further, she flew off the Admiral in one of her aircraft for the last fifty miles to Colombo.

The North Atlantic was exceptionally rough in mid-February, but no one complained. U-Boats would be powerless in such weather. There were, in fact, very few of them about. Most at this time were fitting out in the French west coast ports before moving across the Atlantic to take advantage of the extension of the war to American waters, which were to prove a rich hunting ground over the next three months.

Mr J. J. Curtin, Prime Minister of Australia, many of whose troops were fighting in North Africa when the Japanese began their campaign in Asia, lost no time in asking for these units to be relieved and withdrawn as soon as possible to Australia, where it seemed likely they would be needed for Home Defence. Churchill jibbed at first, but the request had the fullest sympathy of everyone, and as soon as it was possible the 7th Australian Division was embarked for home. There had been some attempt to have part of the division diverted to Rangoon, but the Australian Government was understandably firm. The 16th and 17th Brigades were in Ceylon at the moment, encamped near Colombo, waiting for transport for Australia. So also was the 24th East African Brigade, bound for Burma but not scheduled to arrive there until much later, as well as the major part of the 34th Indian Division. Ceylon's own defence force, the Ceylon Light Infantry and the Ceylon Garrison Artillery, lacked modern weapons, and consisted only of a few units.

It was in the air that Ceylon was to receive most effective

Racecourse and runway (outlined) in the middle of Colombo's suburb of Cinnamon Gardens. This photo \[whic\]h, taken in late 1942, shows camouflage by painting houses, roads, trees etc. on the top end of the runway.

\[...\]Fort, Colombo's city centre, with the harbour in the background. The Galle Face Green, on which Pilot Officer \[Mac\]donald landed his damaged Hurricane, runs beside the shore at the left. The aircraft are Lockheed Hudsons.

Lieutenant-Commander Mitsuo Fuchida, leader of the Pearl Harbour raid and the attacks on Colombo and Trincomalee.

Flight-Lieutenant S. R. Peacock-Edwards, DFC.

Japanese Zero fighters ready for take-off on the flight-deck. All engines are running and auxiliary fuel tanks are fitted below the fuselages.

re-inforcement. Before March no modern planes at all were available in this theatre of war. Old biplanes such as Wapitis and Vildebeestes were still in service here and in India, and the demands of the West and Middle East had made it impossible to replace these. However that month two squadrons of Hurricanes, Nos 30 and 261, were brought over from North Africa in the carrier *Indomitable,* which in the energetic and almost frantic efforts being made to ensure that Ceylon would have a sufficient force of fighter aircraft was, at this juncture, made simply to go to and fro at full speed ferrying aircraft and their equipment.

The two squadrons were earmarked for Java, but Admiral Layton, putting an extremely liberal interpretation on his wide new powers, ordered their diversion to Ceylon. After leaving Singapore and before his arrival at Colombo, Sir Geoffrey Layton had spent a few weeks in Java organising a Naval Headquarters there, so that his expressed opinion that the Hurricanes could help very little in Java and that they would inevitably be lost in the coming débâcle was founded on better intelligence than was available to the Air Ministry, whose vociferous objections were immediately provoked by his action in diverting the fighters. However, his contention that they would be of far greater use in Ceylon was to be fully borne out in the coming weeks.

Seven miles south of Colombo, and only just inland from the west coast, which almost along its entirety is just as Westerners envisage a tropical sea shore, with coconut palms overhanging the golden sand and a long, steady surf combing in from the warm Indian Ocean, is Ratmalana (literally in Singhalese 'the red flower place') and Colombo's Civil Airport was then situated there. It still exists for local and Indian flights, but Katunayake,[1] 18 miles north of Colombo, is now Ceylon's International Airport.

Every tourist who has ever visited Ceylon knows the Mount Lavinia Hotel, close by Ratmalana, on its splendid promontory over the sea.

The metalled runway was rather on the short side, but extension work was immediately put in hand and by the end of the year its length was almost doubled. The Airport was now to lose its civilian

---

[1] Re-named Bandaranaike Airport, constructed by Canada under the Colombo Plan.

status and the RAF moved in. A charming villa in its spacious garden (in Ceylon it is referred to as an 'upstair bungalow'). 'Kandawala', belonging to Colonel Kotelawala, was commandeered as Station Headquarters. As Sir John Kotelawala, its owner was to become Ceylon's second Prime Minister after Independence.

Coconut plantations surrounded the aerodrome which made excellent camouflage and cooling shade, and amongst these quarters for personnel were quickly put up. Most of the buildings, on cement floors, were merely of *kadjan,* the plaited fronds from the coconut palm, on rough round timber, but were comfortable enough for all that in the unfailing warmth and allowed the welcome sea breezes to blow through.

Thirty Squadron, with their Hurricanes, fresh from the North African desert, moved in. No 11 Squadron, with Blenheim medium bombers, veterans from Greece, Crete and the Middle East, had arrived a little earlier, on February 28th. They too settled in at Ratmalana.

No 258 Squadron, virtually a new Squadron, reformed with Hurricanes and much new personnel after service in Malaya with Buffaloes, went at first to Ratmalana, but then moved to the new Racecourse Airstrip and were most comfortably housed in surrounding bungalows in Colombo's fashionable Cinnamon Gardens. The squadron, according to its CO, Squadron Leader P. C. Fletcher (himself a Rhodesian) 'was really international. There may have been two pilots from the U.K., but I think it was only one. The rest came from Australia, New Zealand, Rhodesia, Canada, the United States,[1] South Africa and the Argentine.'

Pilots of No 261, posted to China Bay on the East Coast had, like No 30 Squadron, as untried landlubbers, taken off from the *Indomitable* and flown the last 50 miles or so to the Ceylon coast. One pilot, Sergeant Whittaker, who developed engine trouble after take-off, had even managed to land back on the carrier, an extremely difficult feat, since no arrestor gear was fitted to his Hurricane.

Two squadrons of Fleet Air Arm Fulmars (Nos. 803 and 806)

[1] The American (F/O. Donahue) did not arrive till 18th April.

also reached Ratmalana during March, having flown by stages overland from Alexandria. These two squadrons, then flying Hurricanes, had close ties with No 30 Squadron, RAF, with whom they had composed No 269 Wing, based on the Alexandria area and charged with the air defence of Egypt itself. They were not best pleased at being re-equipped with the slower, far less manoeuvrable, 2-seat Fulmar after handing over their Hurricanes to other units for continued use in the desert.

Across Ceylon, on the East Coast, which has always been less populated than the West, being in the Dry Zone, and less fertile, lies the harbour of Trincomalee, a large natural harbour, entered through a narrow strait from Koddiar Bay, itself reasonably protected from the open sea, and capable of taking the largest fleet in its safe anchorage. Nelson as a young midshipman of 16, called here in the Seahorse in 1775 and thought it the finest natural harbour in the world. It abounds with small bays and inlets, with names which call to mind the many nationalities who have used 'Trinco' in the past. Yard Cove, Back Bay, French Pass, Malay Cove, Clappenberg Bay and Dead Man's Cove.

The aerodrome is named after a large neighbouring sector of the harbour, China Bay, though it immediately abuts on Malay Cove, where Catalina Flying Boats of the Dutch 321 Squadron were later to operate. Immediately inland of the airfield is the shallow, almost land-locked Tambalagam Bay (a Tamil name, this).

China Bay became a hive of activity in March 1942. The station had been well built and designed on an RAF peace-time basis, with airmen's barracks, messes, headquarters, hangars etc. solidly constructed for permanence. Almost all are still standing in good condition in the occupation of the Ceylon Air Force. The Officers' Mess and quarters were on a low hill, immediately south of the airfield and commanded an excellent view all round, both inland across Tambalagam Bay and seawards. North of the aerodrome, and partly concealed by the surrounding jungle are huge fuel storage tanks, then belonging to the Royal Navy.

No 261 (Hurricane) Squadron had served in India for some time and in 1940, when equipped with Gladiators, they had earned some fame at Malta when the island depended entirely on its three surviving planes, christened Faith, Hope and Charity. They flew into China Bay from the *Indomitable* on 25th March.

A strange hotch-potch unit, No 273 Squadron, was also coming into being at China Bay, its flying personnel being largely naval and marine, although it was an RAF unit. To such lengths were we going to muster every effective flying machine for the trial of strength that was to come. It would shortly become a front-line Hurricane squadron, but at the time of which we write it had Fulmars as well as a few other aircraft types. There was one old Seal bi-plane and three FAA pilots had flown in in American-built Martlet fighters. Alas there was insufficient .5 inch ammunition for their guns and they had to be dispersed out of the way. The RAF used .303 ammunition.

From spare aircraft and re-inforcements from the UK, a Swordfish Squadron, No. 788, of the Fleet Air Arm, was also formed at China Bay. This aircraft (always referred to as a 'Stringbag') was a slow biplane, still much in use as a front-line torpedo-bomber by the Navy, though very much out-moded in performance and vulnerability.

At Koggala, a land-locked lagoon just south of the old Dutch Fort of Galle, on Ceylon's south-west coast, a small force of Catalina long-range flying boats was now to complete the complement of No 222 Group RAF and the Ceylon contingent of Naval Air Stations, Eastern Theatre.

These American-built aircraft proved themselves highly dependable work-horses of the air. They were roomy and were equipped with bunks, an electric stove and other comforts, all of which alleviated conditions for crews flying long hours on patrol. The Catalina did this job so efficiently that it was not superseded throughout the war years. One model was amphibious, having an undercarriage which could be retracted into the hull. Never a glamorous plane, it was highly dependable and is remembered by those who had to fly it with affection.

As early as December 1941, soon after Pearl Harbour, four Catalinas of No 202 Squadron, then based at Gibraltar, were sent off in great haste to provide a small long-range reconnaissance flight at Singapore. Koggala was the last stop before the last leg of an extremely long flight. Here the four flying boats had put down during the last week of December, and here they learned that one boat was to remain and be solely responsible for the Ceylon theatre. Singapore would have to make do with the other three.

In deciding who should remain the Flight Commander was helped by the fact that one Captain was Australian and understandably keen to move on in the direction of home.

Flight Lieutenant D. H. T. (Toby) Hildyard, in the end, stayed behind. He is still alive to-day as a result. He has just retired as Britain's Permanent Representative to the United Nation's bodies at Geneva, having been British Ambassador to Chile for some years. The other crews all perished, flying various operations from Singapore.

When the one precious Catalina at Koggala was undergoing inspection or repairs, only a Walrus was available. This was a small single-engined flying-boat and a pusher-type biplane, whose limited range made her a ridiculous substitute, but Hildyard and his co-pilot flew several patrols in the Walrus, as well as flying the Catalina with a full crew when it was serviceable.

Though British air resources were now being stretched to the limit, essential reconnaissance from Ceylon could scarcely be entrusted to a single vulnerable crew; so further re-inforcements had to be found.

No 240 Squadron was based at Lough Erne in Northern Ireland from which it had played an important part in the sighting and shadowing of the German pocket-battleship *Bismarck* in mid-1941. When Singapore was threatened, orders were given for three Catalinas to be detached from North Atlantic duties and urgently despatched to the Far East, though by the time they left, on 23rd February, Singapore had fallen. After delays en route (they were commandeered for various jobs in the Mediterranean) the three flying-boats finished up at Koggala on 9th March. Here a single Catalina of No 205 Squadron had managed to reach safety from Singapore, Flight Lieutenant 'Jock' Graham being her Captain.

For the remainder of the month the three 240 Squadron flying boats and the single boats from 202 and 205 Squadrons flew search patrols at great intensity from Koggala as it was believed that a Japanese sortie was imminent.

Two more eventful flights were flown in March.

In an atmosphere of the greatest secrecy Hildyard flew a party to

Nancowry in the Nicobar Islands, charged with the demolition of installations and supplies on the island and the evacuation of personnel. Fuel stocks were set ablaze, bombs were dumped into the sea and huts were smashed up and burned, but although no less than 23 men, mostly Indians, were crowded into the flying boat, a dozen or so had to be left behind, protesting vociferously. Such foodstuffs and stores as were available were left with them and in the event the Japanese landed and took over within a fortnight.

On the second flight Flight Lieutenant Graham sighted and attacked a Japanese submarine south east of Ceylon on 31st March. To his chagrin there were no explosions and it was found that the fusing links by which, at the moment of separation from the aircraft the depth charges become fused, had fallen with the depth charges, thus leaving them 'safe' and unfused.

All the units we have referred to constituted the major part of air re-inforcements received in the Asian theatre, and their concentration in Ceylon, which left India almost bereft of planes, although causing a good deal of heart-searching at the time, proved to be a wise measure.

CHAPTER FIVE

The First Blows Fall

'With these forces, Vice-Admiral Nagumo is to seek out
and destroy British Sea Power in the Indian Ocean.'
C-IN-C,
JAPANESE COMBINED FLEET.

The idea had become firmly fixed in the official mind that to
concentrate ships together in a poorly defended port presented far
greater risks than to scatter them across the ocean, although
merchant shipping adhering to the recognised sea routes were little
less vulnerable and, once located, were almost helpless. A
devastating attack by Nagumo's carrier-borne flyers, supported by
land-based bombers from the Celebes, on Port Darwin, in
Northern Australia, on 19th February had resulted in the loss of 12
ships. There were too many such harbours where anti-aircraft
defences were sparse and where air protection, if fighters existed at
all, was quite incapable of beating off an attack in any strength.
The Admiralty had therefore ordered that if a threat of
carrier-borne attack developed in the Indian Ocean the principal
ports, especially Calcutta, Madras, Trincomalee and Colombo,
were to be cleared of shipping in good time. In all these ports there
were valuable targets as March drew to a close. In Calcutta alone
over 250,000 tons of merchant shipping was concentrated, much of
it from Singapore and Rangoon. Everyone now expected the
Japanese to take full advantage of the naval supremacy they had so
swiftly won and to harry the Indian Ocean.

As soon as the immediate threat was appreciated, the harbours
of India and Ceylon were cleared. All ships capable of raising steam
were ordered to move out. There were quite a few, of course, who
could not obey the order and had to stay where they were; but over
70 ships were got away from Calcutta.

The *Autolycus* (China Mutual Steam Navigation Co., 7,621
tons, Captain R. C. Neville) was busy loading a general cargo at
Calcutta. She had sailed from England in January with cargo for

Singapore and been diverted, firstly to Rangoon and then to
Calcutta. She and five other ships were ordered to suspend loading
cargo and put out to sea. They sailed on 4th April.

Two days earlier the *Dardanus* (Ocean Steamship Co., 7,725
tons, Captain A. English) had sailed in ballast for Colombo,
accompanied at first by one Greek and one Norwegian vessel, but
later the three ships dispersed and sailed independently. Once clear
of the Ganges delta, a single Japanese 'bomber' (probably a
long-ranged Type 97, 4-Engined Flying Boat from the Andamans)
made an attack on shipping anchored off the pilot station on 3rd
April, but did no worthwhile damage. Her task, clearly, was to
reconnoitre and report. Admiral Ozawa's intention was to sink
what shipping he could find. He first had to locate them.

Vice-Admiral Sir Geoffrey Arbuthnot, C-in-C East Indies
Station, gave similar orders in Colombo and 48 ships weighed
anchor, mostly on the evening of 4th April. They scattered off the
west and north west coast of Ceylon lying at intervals of a few miles
looking, as one airman reported, 'like beads on a necklace'. But 21
merchantmen and 8 Fleet Auxiliaries had to take their chance in
the harbour.

At Trincomalee the few ships there were naval vessels, though
one merchantman the *Sagaing* (whose cargo has ever since been said
to have consisted of whiskey) was at anchor in the centre of the
harbour and for one reason or another was not moved. There was
after all a squadron of Hurricanes available only half a mile away at
China Bay.

Another merchantman, the *Orestes* (Ocean Steam Ship Co., 7,748
Tons, Captain T. B. Marsham) was proceeding southwards after
the exodus from Calcutta when she was attacked three times by a
flying boat (recognised as such and clearly another 'Mavis' from
the Andamans). The ship used her 12-pounder gun with skill and
resolution and Captain Marsham was confident that this kept the
pilot from pressing home his attacks resolutely. A likely alternative
is that he had no more bombs. The *Orestes* was fortunately
undamaged, for if she had been disabled in this particular position
she would certainly have been caught later by Ozawa's cruisers.

The first casualty of the battle to follow fell to a Japanese
submarine of the Second Submarine Flotilla, scouting out the scene

of operations ahead of Nagumo's fleet. The *Glenshiel* (Glen Line, 9,415 tons, Captain R. Brown) had left Karachi and put in at Bombay on its way to Australia. Two days out from Bombay, on 28th March, she picked up a message from Colombo ordering all British ships to return to the port they had last left.

After some hesitation, and after picking up a repetition of the order, Captain Brown turned back. It was later established that the order was for a particular ship and not a general one. The *Glenshiel* therefore resumed course southwards. But for the delay the wireless message had caused her, she would have been well clear of trouble in good time. As it was, at 2.30 a.m. on 3rd April a torpedo passed ahead of her and a second hit her on the port quarter. With the helm jammed, the engines stopped and the ship holed, 'Emergency Stations' were called and by 4 a.m. she was abandoned. The Japanese submarine then surfaced and finally, after two more torpedoes had failed to send her to the bottom, sank the *Glenshiel* with gunfire.

There were 100 passengers on board, including 5 women. But not a soul, it was found, had been lost. The sea was reasonably smooth, it being a month or so before the onset of the south-west monsoon, but their situation was parlous indeed. Adrift over 500 miles from the Ceylon coast, they were on a sea route which was little frequented, even in peace time.

To their great joy and surprise, however, at 5.30 that evening, all were picked up by the destroyer HMS *Fortune*.

For in waters which they felt sure must now be deserted, a large British fleet was in fact on hand.

The Admiralty had been perfectly well alive to the ugly prospect that the Japanese Navy would now move westward even though, as was ultimately to happen, their main trial of strength would be against the Americans in the Pacific. The Admiralty had therefore set their energies to assembling from every possible quarter a fleet which would discourage the Japanese; might even inflict severe losses on them and turn them back for good.

The only battleship of any modernity which was available (and the Admiralty was still battleship-minded) was the *Warspite*, laid down early in World War I, but much modernised and with an armoured deck added. The carrier *Indomitable* was already in the area, having completed her ferrying of Hurricane fighters, and had a complement of Swordfish aircraft. So was the much smaller *Hermes,* though she was due to leave shortly for Australia. She was the first ship ever to be designed as an aircraft-carrier and first saw service just after World War I ended. The light cruisers *Dragon, Caledon, Emerald* and *Enterprise* joined the Eastern Fleet, as it was to be termed. Two rather more modern cruisers, the *Dorsetshire* and *Cornwall,* completed Sir James Somerville's force. Less than a year before, the *Dorsetshire,* then with Captain B. C. S. Martin in command, had fired the final torpedoes into the stricken *Bismarck* in mid-Atlantic. Six destroyers were also on the strength and the Fleet was augmented by two Dutch ships, the *Heemskerk,* a cruiser, and *Isaac Sweers,* a destroyer.

To make up the numbers of this quite useful Fleet, four R Class battleships (*Resolution, Revenge, Ramillies* and *Royal Sovereign*) under Vice-Admiral Sir Algernon Willis were ordered to join. Until recently the Admiralty had been giving serious consideration to having these old battleships scrapped, for they were rather slow and had not been modernised to any great extent since they had been built for service in the First World War. But the heavy losses we had been suffering had made such a course unthinkable. (Apart from those lost in the Far East the *Valiant* and *Queen Elizabeth* had recently been put out of commission by Italian skin-divers at Alexandria and the carrier *Ark Royal* and the battleship *Barham* had been lost). Having no armoured decks the 4 Rs were very vulnerable from the air.

Admiral Somerville, as has been mentioned, had reached Colombo on 24th March. The *Warspite,* which had sailed from America, only arrived on the 26th and the R Class battleships were not to appear on the scene till a week later. Somerville was thus deprived of the necessary time to get his ships together as a fighting combination. Not only the airmen to be involved in the coming struggle, but the sailors too, were flung post haste into the line to find their feet as best they could, knowing little of what was required of them, serving under strange commanders and uncertain of the strategic situation or from where support and co-operation would come.

For once, as Captain Agar has recorded and as all authorities confirm, we knew fairly accurately what was to come. Sir James Somerville immediately decided to put to sea and made his plans on the basis that the enemy would approach from the south-east.

Unknown to the Japanese, and for that matter to most of us in Ceylon, a secret emergency naval base had been set up some time before at Addu Atoll, a remote coral island at the southernmost point of the Maldive Islands. It was some 600 miles South-West of Ceylon. The anchorage was far from perfect, being a large lagoon, not entirely sheltered from the sea, but there were adequate supplies here and its great value lay in the fact that its presence was unsuspected.

Colombo harbour is comparatively small, and has the disadvantage that it is generally crowded with merchant ships. Trincomalee was a better bet, but both would almost certainly be subjected to early enemy attack. Admiral Somerville decided therefore to base the fleet temporarily at Addu Atoll. It was a wise decision indeed. It was here that the 4 Rs, with six more destroyers rendezvoused with the Fleet on the 31st.

Probably because no one knew at that stage that Admiral Nagumo's force had sailed from the Celebes, and not from Singapore, several days sailing time nearer, 31st March was the day on which everyone, including the C-in-C, seems to have expected the Japanese to strike. So narrow had been the margin by which a fleet had been mustered to meet them.

Somerville transferred his flag to the *Warspite*.

Since the enemy did not materialise they were able to spend the 1st and 2nd April in joint manoeuvres, by which time some of the smaller ships and the R Class battleships, which had not been designed for long range work in tropical seas, were in need of fuel and fresh water supplies. There is no doubt that, by the evening of 2nd April, there was a strong feeling that the whole thing might have been a false alarm.

The 8" cruiser *Dorsetshire* had actually started a refit at Colombo towards the end of March, with engines to be dismantled, boilers scraped etc.; but when the alarm was sounded had hurriedly discontinued this and joined the Fleet.

She was now ordered to return to Colombo to resume her refit. With her went her sister ship, the *Cornwall*, due to escort to

Australia a convoy, SU 4, which was expected from the Middle East with Australian troops and which would pick up the brigades now at Colombo. The *Hermes,* whose boilers also needed cleaning, was despatched to Trincomalee with the destroyer *Vampire.* This small and rather ancient vessel had been with the *Prince of Wales* and *Repulse* on their last voyage. These two ships were due to take part in operations planned shortly against Madagascar (Operation Ironclad).

The remainder of the Fleet put back to Addu Atoll for refuelling and tension seems slightly to have relaxed. A careful eye was kept eastwards, however. Swordfish flew air searches and a light screen of destroyers patrolled the seas well forward of the area. It was one of these, the *Fortune,* which came upon the *Glenshiel's* survivors.

Admiral Nagumo at midnight on the 2nd was well into the Indian Ocean, with the coast of Sumatra left some 500 miles to the north-east of his Fleet. Admiral Ozawa, with his Malaya Force from Mergui was marking time to synchronise with Nagumo his entry into the Bay of Bengal. His Force, consisting of seven cruisers and the light aircraft carrier *Ryujo,* with attendant destroyers, was equipped to clear the seas of any merchant shipping they might come across. Nagumo had a more vital task to carry out – to find and destroy what remained of British Sea Power in the East.

His intelligence indicated that British naval strength was fast building up in the Indian Ocean and the Bay of Bengal. He was ordered to smash this enemy strength and warned at the same time that he might have to face more than 300 British and Indian Air Force planes in Ceylon and along the Bay of Bengal. From the naval point of view this intelligence was true enough, though this grossly exaggerated the air situation. Our air defences were scattered over an enormous area and were mostly of out-of-date type and poor performance. Nagumo had 300 aircraft of his own, concentrated under his immediate command as a massive striking force. Wherever it struck the British could put up, at the very most, one tenth of the Japanese First Air Fleet's numbers – generally less.

Nagumo expected to find the British ships at Trincomalee or Colombo, or in Ceylon waters, and was confident that if they could be located he had more than sufficient forces at his disposal to carry out his orders to the letter.

The First Air Fleet, save for the absence of the carrier *Kaga*, despatched to Japan for repairs and supplies, was as it had been when they had attacked Pearl Harbour four months before. It consisted of the five aircraft-carriers, *Akagi* (in which Nagumo flew his flag), *Shokaku, Zuikaku, Hiryu* and *Soryu*, each carrying a complement of from 36 to 54 light bombers and 18 Zero fighters; four battleships, the *Kongo, Hiei, Kirishima* and *Haruna*; the heavy cruisers *Tone* and *Chikuma*; the light cruiser *Abukama,* and eleven destroyers. There were also seven Japanese submarines operating in the Indian Ocean at the time. As it happens the battleships were just as old as Admiral Somerville's, though much modernised and rather faster. But their role was to be a minor one.

In terms of numbers and tonnage, Nagumo's supremacy over his adversary was not so great except in the crucial matter of aircraft and aircraft carriers where he was in an utterly commanding situation.

Thrown thus hastily and haphazardly together, the real value of the British Eastern Fleet amounted to much less than the sum total of its component units.

To Nagumo the converse applied. He was able to call on incalculable extra strength provided by lengthy combined training, a string of unqualified successes, mutual confidence between every echelon and many other intangible spiritual qualities in which the Japanese were naturally indoctrinated. Thus the total value of Nagumo's force much exceeded the sum total of its available components. Furthermore he had an inestimable advantage in that the initiative was his, that his force could therefore be kept together as a whole and that he would choose where and when to strike.

To this extent he was in a much happier position than Admiral Somerville who knew that after the Battle of the Java Seas he had the only' ships available in the Indian Ocean for the protection of the all-important route to the Middle East from the Cape up the East African coast along which, in the reverse direction, essential oil supplies had to be brought. He was sure this Fleet was inferior to what could be brought against him by the Japanese. He could therefore afford to lose none of this force. According to Captain Agar;

A defeat would uncover these routes and lay open the way, not only for the invasion of India (where there were no defences worth considering) but also cut us off from the Middle East until the position could be restored. The risk of seeking combat was one which he simply could not accept. Added to this he had that morning [26th March] received a personal cypher message from the First Sea Lord [Sir Dudley Pound], which he showed me, in which he was most strongly advised not to allow his Fleet to become engaged with anything except inferior forces until the Eastern Fleet could be re-inforced.

Captain Agar adds drily:

The First Sea Lord was in the habit of sending these personal messages to our Flag Officers when conducting operations and they were obviously intended to influence their judgment and decisions. (How fortunate for Britain that Wireless Telegraphy was not invented at the time of the Nile, Copenhagen and Trafalgar!)

In the event Somerville decided that the only offensive action he could contemplate would be a night torpedo attack. This would have to be delivered by his Fleet Air Arm units which, on the voyage from Greenock to Colombo, he had been at pains to train to this work.

In one such practice strike carried out during the first few days of March in the South Atlantic, Lieutenant Mike Lithgow, who had also flown from the *Ark Royal* in the *Bismarck* hunt, flying an Albacore had found himself caught in the slipstream of a number of other planes, all flying very low over the water. Momentarily thrown off balance his plane crashed into the sea. Both he and his two fellow crew members managed to get clear and were kept afloat by one of the aircraft's wheels, wrenched off in the crash.

They were thus left in mid-Atlantic, at dead of night. They knew quite well that it would be some time before they would be missed, for none of their fellow flyers had witnessed their plight. Furthermore the carrier was steaming away from them, increasing the distance between them with every moment that passed. Even if the carrier turned back to search, they constituted only the smallest speck in the ocean.

Admiral Somerville in the *Formidable* thought it unlikely the missing crew could ever be located, but ordered the ship about to search for them.

Several hours later, still in darkness, the carrier passed sufficiently close to the three men for their cries to be heard and they were picked up.

In his foreword to Lithgow's book, *Mach One* (Allan Wingate) Charles Gardner, who is later to play a part in this story, describes the odds against such a thing happening as about the same as for picking up all the trumps in one bridge hand. This cannot be much of an exaggeration.

With a night torpedo attack the only action he could contemplate against the Japanese, Admiral Somerville was faced with keeping his heavy fleet units out of the way, though available if needed, and following the enemy's moves by aerial reconnaissance.

The practical range of his Swordfish and Albacore aircraft for this purpose was less than 200 miles, so the intelligence he needed would have to be supplied by the RAF Catalinas in Ceylon. These were capable of up to 30 hours endurance.

Owing to the need for overhauling and maintenance, much overdue after their long flights out, only one of the 240 Squadron Catalinas was serviceable at this moment. A Dutch Catalina was also available at Koggala flown by Lieutenant Hamers, but this was earmarked for an important communications flight to Addu Atoll, since it was considered absolutely essential to maintain strict radio silence and there was no other means of keeping in touch with the Eastern Fleet.

However the authorities had not lost sight of the enormous importance of long range reconnaissance, of which only these flying boats were capable, and others were due to arrive in the nick of time.

The one serviceable 240 Squadron Catalina was L for Lionel, which had a patch in her hull where the *Bismarck's* guns had holed her. Her Captain was Flight Lieutenant W. (Bill) Bradshaw, DFC, with Pilot Officer Charles Gardner, at one time well known as a BBC broadcaster, as her second pilot. For sixteen hours on the

following day they flew an extended search eastwards but drew a
blank. Meanwhile the much needed flying boat reinforcements
were appearing on the scene.

No 413 (Canadian) Squadron was stationed until early March at
Sullom Voe in the Shetland Islands with the chill seas north of the
British Isles as their field of operations. During the winter Sullom
Voe is a grey, cheerless place with the sun not rising much before
ten o'clock and setting at three. At this stage the squadron's
personnel was only partly Canadian, partly British. Its temporary
squadron commander, on the departure of the previous
commander for an Air Ministry appointment, was Squadron
Leader L. J. Birchall, from St. Johns, New Brunswick, and under
his leadership a detachment moved in early March to Pembroke
Dock on the Welsh Coast to fit themselves out for tropical
operations. Ground crews sailed from Liverpool and did not catch
up with the Squadron until May, when our story will have been
told.

No 413 was now entrusted with an unusual task.

We have mentioned earlier on that General Sir Archibald Nye,
Deputy Chief of the Imperial General Staff, was to be sent by the
Prime Minister to Cairo to confer with Sir Claude Auchinleck. As a
matter of interest, Nye himself had been considered by Churchill as
a possible successor to the post of C-in-C Middle East. Despatched
at very short notice, the General was taken aboard the first of 413
Squadron's Catalinas to be got ready (Y for Yorker), its course
scheduled to take them out into the Atlantic, well clear of hostile
territory, to Gibraltar and then on to Cairo. For the latter leg much
of the flight would need to be at 'nought feet' to avoid radar
coverage.

After an abortive start when the aircraft was recalled from the
Atlantic owing to bad weather at Gibraltar to a tricky night landing
at Lough Erne in Ulster, its crew, under Flight Lieutenant Rae
('Tommy') Thomas, DFC, a South African from Cape Town, set out
again. General Nye has said, 'I think I can fairly say that the
aircraft had the most efficient crew which I have met.' He was
impressed by the navigation (the navigator, Flying Officer R. E.
Hervey was Canadian). 'I remember,' he recalls, 'that they even
went to the trouble of preparing a small menu card for our meals

and produced very substantial meals as well.'

After dropping General Nye at Alexandria, Thomas and his crew flew on to Basra, Karachi and finally Koggala. The lagoon was far from ideal as a flying-boat base as it had various obstructions in it and the only stretch of clear water was on the short side. Thomas's CO, Squadron Leader Birchall followed him out as soon as indifferent weather at Pembroke Dock would allow. Another Catalina, under Flight Lieutenant O. G. Roberts, completed the trip out from Wales at much the same time, and some Dutch crews arrived exhausted from the Dutch East Indies and were the forerunners of others who were formed later into No 321 (Dutch) Squadron to be based in Malay Cove at Trincomalee.

Thus, in the nick of time – Birchall arrived only on 2nd April – was a small but invaluable force of long range reconnaissance planes made available for the Eastern Fleet and Ceylon's defenders.

Thomas and his crew (7 all told) made a lengthy flight eastwards on 1st April without sighting anything and flew a similar patrol on the 3rd. Their line of flight, east-south-east of Ceylon, was in fact farther north than the actual Japanese line of approach.

After spending the 3rd shaking down in their new surroundings, Squadron Leader Birchall's men were able to take a hand.

Though they should have had the chance of making a few dusk and night landings on the lake to familiarise themselves with the difficult conditions, the urgency of the situation forbade this and at about six o'clock on the morning of 4th April, with a maximum fuel load to keep them airborne right through until daylight on the 5th and thus obviate a night landing, Birchall took off with orders to patrol throughout the daylight hours an area 250 miles south-east of the island. Because of rigid wireless silence our own fleet's movements were not known and they were told to report on all ships seen, whether friendly or hostile. Their last patrol, just over a month ago, had been in the chill area north of the Shetland Islands.

They had not yet spent two days in the highly contrasting conditions at Koggala, and yet here they were over tropical waters with a strange new enemy opposed to them. The sun rose as they approached the patrol area. For hour after hour there was only empty sea below them. Shipping routes came nowhere near here, and in any event they were now in no-man's-land. During the day they received a coded wireless message to switch their patrol well to the south.

In conditions such as this the navigator's task is a hard one. Warrant Officer 'Bart' Onyette (Canadian) had to rely on dead-reckoning, with no land-marks of any sort, and astro-navigation. With only the sun available, it was not possible to confirm their positions accurately. About two hours before their daylight patrol was to finish (at dusk), the moon was due to rise and this would provide an excellent fix from combined sun and moon shots.

They continued on to the southernmost point of their search and Onyette got his fix, placing them almost 350 miles south-south-east of Ceylon – much further south than an enemy approach would normally be considered likely.

Birchall and his crew now began to work out a course back to base, when they noticed a small speck on the extreme southern horizon. As they had sufficient fuel to keep them airborne until the following dawn, they turned south to investigate. It was surprising to find any ship at all in such a position but it seemed possible it might be a Royal Naval vessel. At 2,000 feet, at which height they would get a detailed view of anything on the surface, they flew towards the object and as they got close enough to attempt identification of the ship, they found that it was only the precursor of a huge fleet of battleships, carriers, destroyers and supply ships, which now hove into view.

This was obviously the expected Japanese fleet and they were now in the gravest peril. It may well be imagined how slender are the chances of a slow, heavy flying boat ever returning to base to augment its wireless report when within visual distance of a powerful force such as this, with its deadly complement of carrier-borne fighters, and the moment the Catalina had been sighted by the Japanese 6 Zeros were flown off the *Hiryu* to deal with it.

A first sighting report, giving the fleet's composition, course and estimated speed, in the standard code, had now to be sent to base. Sergeant Phillips hastily began his transmission as Birchall turned northwards at maximum speed. There was no cloud cover and the old 'Cat', at full boost, was only capable of 180 m.p.h. The six Zero fighters could fly almost twice as fast. They were sighted coming up from astern. Two members of the crew swung out their two side blister guns, prepared to hit back.

Sergeant Phillips got his message away and quickly began a repetition. Regulations required it to be repeated three times. As he began the first repetition the Zeros struck.

One of the Hurricane pilots, just arrived in Ceylon, has said, 'We knew nothing of the Japanese; neither their aircraft nor their tactics.' The Catalina's crew will have known no better.

The armament of the Zero consisted of 2 x .303 inch machine guns and 2 x 20 mm. cannon, firing small explosive shells. The .303 bullet, similar to those fired by the Hurricanes then in Ceylon, had to find a vulnerable target to disable a plane. Time and again it had been found possible for an aircraft to receive numerous hits from the .303 gun, yet fly on. The cannon shell, however, exploding on impact, was a terribly effective weapon. Several Zeros, swooping down on the lumbering flying-boat, began to send these shells thudding into her. Phillips was half way through his third transmission when one hit the wireless equipment, completely destroying it. Another shattered the leg of Sergeant Calorossi, one of the blister gunners.

The Japanese knew they must destroy the flying-boat as swiftly as possible, before the Fleet's presence could be reported. They pressed home their attacks ruthlessly. Internal fuel tanks in the Catalina began to blaze. Crew members managed to get the fire out with extinguishers. All the while Squadron Leader Birchall pressed on, taking what evasive action he could. Enemy attacks were now almost continuous. The internal fire started again. With two of the crew seriously injured she started to break up in the air. The enemy still constantly straffed them and there seemed no escaping destruction. They were 350 miles from land, it was nearly 6 p.m. and darkness was about to fall.

Back in Ceylon the message, a little garbled but essentially correct, was received and passed on to all the Services. Admiral Somerville was informed of it immediately. Rather ominously, he noted, the Japanese fleet was in much the same latitude as Addu Atoll – almost on the Equator. In fact Nagumo had intentionally approached beyond what he considered the limit of likely reconnaissance from Ceylon. If he had made it only a mile or two further to the south he would have escaped detection.

A listening watch was kept all night, but nothing more was heard of Birchall and his crew. When they did not appear at dawn at Koggala they were presumed shot down. Few members of the Catalina detachment had even had the chance to meet the lost crew. 'All I ever saw of Birchall,' said one, 'was his kit, left in a corner of the mess.' Their loss was mourned but at least we now knew where the Japanese fleet were. Calculations were made and it was estimated that Ceylon would be attacked early next morning.

No time was wasted in regaining contact with the enemy ships and darkness had scarcely fallen before Flight Lieutenant Graham in the 205 Squadron Catalina was sent off, armed with the sighting position radioed by Birchall, to shadow the enemy fleet. Between midnight and one a.m. he signalled that he had sighted an enemy destroyer some 200 miles well to the south east of Ceylon, headed north west. Ominously the message was not repeated.

No further word was ever heard from Graham and the eight other members of his crew.

Earlier in the afternoon the cruisers *Dorsetshire* and *Cornwall* had berthed at Colombo and were told that some new ack-ack guns and radar equipment had arrived for them. The *Dorsetshire*'s engineers rolled up their sleeves and started once again on dismantling engines. They had scarcely begun, however, when they were, for the second time in little under a week, ordered to hold everything and rejoin the main Fleet. The ships could not be brought to readiness before 10 p.m. but sailed at that time. It was calculated that the rendezvous appointed by Admiral Somerville, some 100 miles nearer Colombo from Addu Atoll, would take them till 4 p.m. on the 5th to reach.

Admiral Somerville himself, with the *Warspite* and the two carriers, which, with a few of the faster elements of the Fleet, were now to be known as 'Force A', left Addu Atoll at midnight, probing eastwards towards the Japanese. It was miserable luck that at this very moment half his Fleet was immobilised for lack of fuel and water. The slower 'Force B', composed basically of the four old battleships, stayed to refuel.

Designed for short range work in colder home waters, conditions on board these battleships were appalling. It was oppressively hot within their steel sides. Limited water supplies made stringent rationing necessary and neither clothes nor bodies could be washed frequently enough for comfort.

Admiral Somerville's biographer, Captain Donald Macintyre, with access to private correspondence passing between the Admiral and Lady Somerville, as well as to communications addressed to 'their Lordships' at the Admiralty, leaves us in no doubt as to what its newly appointed C-in-C thought of the Fleet.

Although he now had under his command a British naval force 'much bigger than anything anyone else has had to handle before during this war' he had vociferously expressed his dissatisfaction with it, stressing particularly its lack of training. To their Lordships, as well as to Churchill, who expected great things of the Fleet, his reports must have been a bitter disappointment. General Sir Archibald Wavell, the new C-in-C India, also hoped for greater things of the new Fleet than Admiral Somerville felt it could manage; such as a bombardment of Akyab in Northern Burma to assist the withdrawal there. 'I replied I could do nothing until the Fleet was trained and I was not prepared to use it offensively until I was satisfied it was in a proper state.'

From the word go in the North Atlantic, he had considered the *Formidable*'s flyers 'terribly green and inexperienced'. The accident rate was high enough to elicit the comment 'at this rate we shall have hardly any aircraft left by the time we arrive; but it's no good having aircraft if the chaps can't fly them properly.

> My old battle boats are in various states of disrepair and there is not a ship at present that approaches what I should call a proper standard of fighting efficiency.
> This ship [*Formidable*] evidently wants a proper training programme, which I hope to give her as soon as the weather becomes favourable.

When mustering his Fleet on 31st March near Addu Atoll Somerville called it 'collecting all my scattered and untrained boys to see what I can do about it'.

'Everyone,' he commented 'is naturally very rusty about doing their Fleet stuff. Most ships have hardly been in company with another ship since the war.'

Although he undoubtedly kept up an unfailingly optimistic attitude before 'his untrained boys' and even managed to boost their morale at a time when it much needed boosting, this, we now know, is how he really regarded the Eastern Fleet.

Admiral Somerville had built up a great reputation in the Mediterranean where he had shown a splendid offensive spirit against the Italians. The Royal Navy, too, had its great traditions. It is as startling now, therefore, to read the Admiral's comments as it must have been for their Lordships in 1942. Could the entire Fleet be so untrained at this time? After all, the war had been going for $2\frac{1}{2}$ years.

With the Fleet temporarily split, whatever its shortcomings, it was now the turn of Ceylon's air defences to prove their mettle.

The Colombo Racecourse Airstrip being now in full operation, No. 11 (Blenheim) Squadron had moved the necessary few miles to the strip from Ratmalana on the 24th March; and as *Hermes* approached Trincomalee, her Swordfish Squadron (No 814, Fleet Air Arm) was flown off to re-inforce aircraft at China Bay.

In other respects the squadrons were distributed as we have described earlier. Thanks to Birchall's sighting everyone now knew that the following day was *the* day and the position of the Japanese Fleet made it clear that Colombo, on the west coast, would be their target.

To meet the attack, which might well be delivered by over a hundred planes, there were in Colombo and its environs two squadrons of Hurricanes and a few Fleet Air Arm Fulmars. Trincomalee was 160 miles away, so the China Bay Hurricane squadron and the 273 Squadron Fulmars could not be counted on to help. They were out of range.

CHAPTER SIX

Easter Sunday

'I shall never get over this.'

AIR VICE-MARSHAL d'ALBIAC

The 5th April dawned rather cloudy on the west coast. At Ratmalana fighter pilots, ground crews and most others were up at 4 a.m. First light was at about 6 o'clock. Defence positions were manned and all flyers were on 'immediate readiness', with trolley batteries plugged in for an immediate start.

Two routine patrols were flown at first light, the first, of two Hurricanes from 30 Squadron, reported 8/10ths storm clouds over most of the area. The second, a Flight of 6 FAA Fulmars, flew down the west coast and round towards the east, and back again. They flew just below the cloud in battle formation, that is in pairs, keeping a weather eye open.

Colombo is in many ways a spacious city, covering a large area, but not densely. Except for the crowded Pettah, to the north and north-east of the harbour, its houses are well laid out and from the air there always seems to be more tropical greenery than masonry. The centre business sector of the city, which is small, is called the Fort. This immediately adjoins the harbour, as most of the Pettah does, and unless the Japanese bombers used the greatest care, there was every risk of damage here.

Colombo's citizens unsuspectingly prepared for another day. For almost everyone it was a day off. For Christians it was a day of especial significance; for it was Easter Sunday. For this reason, and being comparatively early in the day, the streets of the Fort were almost deserted.

When could the attack be expected?

There were several schools of thought on the question.

A dawn attack was a possibility; but that would mean a difficult night take-off from the carriers. In view of the known position of the

Japanese fleet such an attack would be more likely on the following day, the 6th.

If the enemy planes took off at dawn, they would arrive at about 8 a.m. The bombers could manage the range but not fighters. Our knowledge of the Zero's capabilities at that time seemed to rule out fighter support. In daylight unescorted bombers would be easy meat. To risk them in this way seemed altogether too rash a step for the Japanese to take.

The third course, in order to utilise fighter protection would be to steam closer in to within normal fighter range. In this event the attack could be expected nearer mid-day.

On the Racecourse, No 258 Squadron was in the same state of readiness as No 30 at Ratmalana. They watched and waited. As they waited the clouds began to clear somewhat.

Across the Island, some 160 miles north-east of Colombo, Lieutenant-Commander S. M. de L. (Nipper) Longsdon, CO of the Fleet Air Arm's No. 788 Squadron at China Bay, took off for Colombo at first light, leading a flight of 6 Swordfish, carrying torpedoes. If the Japanese appeared within range off the Western coast, this was the force – rather a pathetic one it now seems – which would attack the enemy ships. Two months before just such a sortie had been made, led by Lieutenant-Commander Esmond, against the *Scharnhorst* and *Gneisenau* in the English Channel and had met with total annihilation, Esmond earning a posthumous Victoria Cross in the attempt.

On Admiral Somerville's flagship a disturbing series of signals began to come in from merchant ships hugging the Eastern coast of India. Between 6.40 and 10.11 a.m. one ship after the other reported being attacked by aircraft or surface vessels. *Bierville, Malda, Silksworth, Sinkuang.* At least one mentioned battleships; incorrectly as it happens.

Ozawa was carefully synchronising his operations with Nagumo's.

At Ratmalana and Colombo Racecourse a watery sun began to show through the broken clouds and anxious eyes continued to scan the heavens.

At a point rather more than 200 miles south of the Island, just before the sun appeared over the horizon, Nagumo's fleet, steaming as close as he dared to come, had reached, at full speed, the appointed take-off area and the first machines roared off into the dawn sky. The force of 125 planes was under the command of Commander Mitsuo Fuchida, of the *Akagi,* who had led the Pearl Harbour attack, one of Japan's most experienced flyers who already counted 25 years service in the Imperial Navy, and was certainly by far the oldest man to be flying that day on either side.

They took to the skies in quick succession from the 5 carriers, as they steamed head-on into the wind. Fuchida felt certain that the enemy Catalina would have had time to send back a sighting report before being shot down. He was ready for trouble. Up to yesterday evening they had had no reason at all to believe they were expected and had hoped to achieve the same surprise as at Pearl Harbour. These hopes, they now realised, were jeopardised. But they could not be sure.

They had more than mere guess-work to go on. For six exhausted survivors of Squadron Leader Birchall's crew, three of them seriously injured, were crammed in the most inhumane conditions into the forward paint locker of the destroyer *Isokaze.*

Field Marshal Sir William Slim, in his book *Defeat into Victory* (Cassell), writes;

'The Japanese conduct to prisoners in the field and in their prison camps will always remain a foul blot on their record, which those who fought against them will find it hard to forget.'

For generations the Japanese soldier had been led to believe, and clearly did so believe, that to die in the service of his country ensured him an honourable place in the life to come. For the leaders of a martial race such a creed had an enormous (and possibly cynical) value. It ensured that feats of the greatest valour would be carried out without hesitation when required. The Kamikaze pilots, who were to figure later on in the war, when desperate times merited desperate measures, flew to their scheduled deaths with a stoicism and patient disregard for their lives which civilised men (and I use the term deliberately) could emulate only under the severest stress in the heat of battle.

Unhappily there was a reverse side to the coin.

Honourable as it was to die for one's country, it was one of the greatest disgraces to avoid death by falling into the hands of the enemy. It was to be months before Japanese prisoners were to be taken by the Americans or the British and, even then, these were men who were unconscious or shocked beyond rational behaviour. Most contemplated suicide and had to be carefully watched if this was to be prevented. The Japanese, therefore, were unable to accord prisoners of war the faintest sympathy, however hard their ordeal.

Though there were many proven instances of even greater cruelty, there could be no better illustration of Sir William Slim's justifiable comment than the treatment meted out to Birchall and his crew.

We in Ceylon were not to hear that some had survived and been picked up by the Japanese until almost a year later.

Birchall recalls; 'The aircraft started to break up in the air. Due to our low altitude it was impossible for us to bail out and I managed to get the aircraft down onto the water before the tail fell off. All the time we were landing and immediately thereafter we were under constant enemy strafing.'

At this stage the three on the flight deck, Birchall himself, Flying Officer Kenny, the 2nd Pilot and Onyette, the navigator, seem to have escaped serious injury. Farther back in the central fuselage, however, the crew had suffered severely. There were more of them than was normal. Two of them had never received formal training as air crew, but had come along as air gunners. These were Sergeant Cook, a Flight Mechanic, and Sergeant Henzell, a Flight Rigger. Apart from Sergeant Phillips, wounded as he got off the all-important sighting report, Sergeant Calorossi, one of the Wireless Operators, had been very badly hit whilst firing one of the guns. Sergeant Catlin, the Engineer, was also wounded. 'During the action I was only aware of being hit once, in the chest, though on my left hand only the little finger would still work. Afterwards, somebody counted the holes in me and scored 74. There were also some burns. Mostly cannon splinters and with few long term effects.'

Once down on the water there was no letting up for the helpless flying boat and her crew, now sitting ducks. The six Zeros still came in, one behind the other, firing with everything they had.

Sergeant Henzell in the front turret was hit and seriously wounded and as Cook and Kenny tried to get him out Cook's leg was shattered by a cannon burst.

Abandoning the sinking aircraft in such conditions was a nightmare. Sergeant Davidson tried valiantly to stay and help his fellow Wireless Operator Calorossi, obviously mortally wounded, but was ordered out. Calorossi and Henzell in the end went down with the plane.

'The remaining seven of us swam away from the burning gasoline which spread out over the water,' says Birchall, 'Once we were away from the aircraft, the strafing still continued and it was necessary for us to dive under the water each time the enemy aircraft fired at us.'

Davidson was in a fully inflated life-jacket which made it almost impossible to dive. This perhaps is the reason for his being hit and killed in the water. 'He had been very steady in the action and was, I think, unwounded until then', says Catlin.

'This left six of us,' recalls Birchall, 'and we continued to stay in a group until the destroyer came over and put out a small boat to pick us up. We were then taken to the destroyer and put on the forward deck.

'Three of the crew were badly injured, both from wounds they had received during the fight and also in the water, and were lying on the deck in a state of semi-consciousness. The other three of us, although we had received several wounds, were fairly well off. The purpose of our being picked up was to find out whether we had been able to send a warning message and, secondly, to obtain any information we had concerning the defences of Ceylon, such as the location of the Royal Navy ships. We immediately denied having gotten a message away and said we had only arrived in Colombo the day before and taken off during the night; therefore we did not have any knowledge of the Ceylon defences. Throughout the questioning we were severely beaten.'

For the Japanese had been listening out on the correct wave-length and realised perfectly well that some message had been sent off. Whether they understood the self-evident code is doubtful and no one could be sure that the transmission had been picked up and understood in Ceylon.

The airmen stuck to their contention that no message had been sent, but when Colombo called up and asked for a repetition and clarification of the message the fat was in the fire and the beatings were redoubled.

As darkness fell the six captives were dragged below. Sergeant Cook, whose leg would later have to be amputated, was as harshly treated as the others. Finally a door was slammed on them in a cramped paint locker in the bows of the destroyer. Here there was room only for three to lie down; two could sit and one had to stand. In these inhuman conditions, with no medical attention and only one cup of soup a day, they were to be kept for the next three days.

Japan did not subscribe to the 1929 Geneva Convention which laid down humane treatment for prisoners of war. To be precise, her representatives had signed the Convention but no formal ratification ever followed. It is hardly surprising therefore that no clear instructions were laid down for the treatment of prisoners by the Japanese Armed Forces. Whatever the spirit of Bushido might have required, however, one might have expected some evidence of that corner-stone of Buddhist philosophy, compassion towards others. But no; their captors seem to have reverted to a mere primitivism in their treatment of these injured and terribly shaken men who, after all, had not even been guilty of any offensive move against them.

At the time of the Battle of Midway, two months later, the Captain of the *Isokaze* was Commander Shunichi Toshima, and it is highly probable that he commanded in April 1942. If so, even at this length of time, one cannot help wishing him suitably ill. The ultimate fate of the *Isokaze* three years later will be mentioned in due course but I have not been able to trace what happened to Commander Toshima.

In all the circumstances the Japanese took the view that Ceylon had been warned of the presence of their Fleet. They now expected opposition.

Fuchida's force was composed of 36 Type 99 Dive Bombers (Vals), each with a crew of two, 53 Type 97 Attack Bombers (Kates), with a crew of three, and an escort of 36 Zero fighters. He himself flew as an observer in one of the Kates, flown by Lieutenant Mitsuo Matsuzaki.

They climbed steadily on course for the south-west coast of the island. After making a landfall they planned to fly well clear of the coast northwards to the capital. The fact that the Zero was capable of flying over 200 miles, spending perhaps 20 minutes in combat and returning the same distance, had hardly been suspected by the Allies at this time. They themselves had nothing to compete with this. Of course it must not be forgotten that it is a great strain on a lone flyer to carry out a mission of such length, including the essential navigation back to his carrier. For this trip the Zeros carried auxiliary fuel tanks which were dropped before Colombo was reached.

Though the erection of one unit near Ratmalana (No. 524 AMES) had only begun on 1st April, Ceylon had modest radar facilities at this time. Exercises and practice raids carried out over the past few weeks had shown that they were sufficient to ensure the defences adequate warning of air attack. On this point everyone was reassured.

Important radar equipment was in course of shipment from Karachi and reinforcements were in the convoy, WS 16. By 5th April the Far East element of this convoy was most of the way across the Indian Ocean on course to Bombay from the Cape. It is unlikely that they were apprised of the Japanese threat.

No one could doubt that the radar posts were very much on the qui vive on Sunday morning. They were linked over commandeered telephone lines with Fighter Operations Headquarters in Colombo.

The huge air armada made its landfall at 7.15 in the Galle area and flew on up the coast for half an hour at a height of some 8,000 feet. Thousands must have seen and heard them. Whether radar picked them up or not was scarcely material for the Hurricanes could have been given half an hour's adequate warning with merely visual aids. No one, however, on the west coast had any reason to believe the planes were not friendly.

It has never been satisfactorily explained why Fighter Operations did not learn of the arrival of the Jap planes until after 30 Squadron had been engaged and No 258 was taking off from the Racecourse. It was said that watches were being changed at the crucial moment and the radar had gone unmanned for some time. Furthermore, since no one realised the great range of the Japanese aircraft, the radar men seem to have clung to the view that their carriers would need to approach much closer and the attack would most likely develop much later in the day. With standby at the aerodromes at the early hour of 4 a.m. such a situation is scarcely credible. The Air Officer Commanding, Air Vice-Marshal d'Albiac, was aghast at the situation. 'I shall *never* get over this,' he was to say later.

He had had unhappy experiences in the war to date. Exactly a year before, as Air Officer Commanding Air Force units in Greece, he had witnessed the destruction of these by the Luftwaffe and the hurried withdrawal to Crete of the surviving remnants. One of these units was 11 Squadron with its Blenheims, though squadron personnel were now much changed.

Failure in communications all round was to bring tragic results in its wake. Afterwards there was even talk of sabotage but this cannot be taken seriously.

The six Fulmars, returning from their dawn patrol, actually sighted some of the enemy planes. Sub-Lieutenant R. V. Hinton in one of the aircraft reported, 'On the return journey, somewhere between Bentota and Colombo, we saw a number of aircraft out to sea some distance away, and fortunately or unfortunately for us, it did not occur to us at the time that they were Japanese. It subsequently transpired that on the fall of the first bomb on Ratmalana, the wireless went dead (not through direct enemy action) and we were therefore not in communication with base. If in fact communication had been maintained, we could have put ourselves in an attacking position as the Japanese aircraft returned, unaware of our presence.'

Surprisingly enough, even earlier than this the Japanese air armada had already been sighted by an RAF air-crew.

When Graham's Catalina had failed to return, assumed like Birchall's shot down by the enemy, the essential need remained of keeping watch on the Japanese warships. The chances of a third flying boat doing so without being destroyed seemed poor indeed, but the men who were detailed to regain contact did not shrink from the unenviable task. They were Flight Lieutenant Bradshaw DFC, and his crew in the 'Bismarck' Catalina from 240 Squadron.

They took off before dawn and flew at 'nought' feet. In this way they reduced the chances of their being picked up by radar. They were not to know that the Japanese had no radar in fact.

On the way out they saw at some distance many planes flying north, far above them, but they had been briefed to expect British carrier-borne planes in the area and, under the assumption that, being so close to Ceylon the aircraft were friendly, did not break wireless silence to report them. They, in turn, were not apparently sighted by the Japanese, so low over the water. So two opportunities of warning the defences were unhappily missed.

Bradshaw's Catalina had not flown south for long before they sighted on the farthest horizon the forward elements of the Japanese fleet; these seemed to be battleships and cruisers, which had moved protectively ahead of the carriers. Turning away unseen, they sent back a sighting report and we knew once more where the enemy fleet lay.

At Ratmalana the sun had climbed some way into the heavens with no indication received of an impending attack. There was now a tendency to feel it may all have been a false alarm after all. At 7.30 some men were released for breakfast. At 7.50, to everyone's horror, the enemy formations appeared overhead. Startled pilots rushed to take off and the alarm was sounded.

In spite of all precautions and in spite of their long vigil No 30 Squadron, under Squadron Leader G. F. Chater, DFC, was caught on the ground, with 8,000 feet to be climbed before the enemy bombers could be reached and, what was much worse, with the protecting fighters in a far superior position. We now know that one of the few advantages the Hurricane had over the Zero was its ability, from its greater weight to out-dive the Zero. Quite apart from this, at no time, regardless of its type, is an aircraft more vulnerable than just after take-off, before full power is developed or speed and altitude gained.

The Hurricane pilots rushed madly to their planes, engines burst into life, breathless youngsters slid into their cockpits and even as the enemy struck Hurricanes began to rumble across the aerodrome into the air.

The Japanese were well aware of the existence of Ratmalana, as it was a civil aerodrome, marked on the maps since before the War. They expected to be met by fighters from this station and were pleased to find them on the ground, or merely climbing into the air below them as the main body flew on. A small force of Type 99 Dive-bombers detached themselves and, in line astern, dived down to release their bombs at about 500 feet. Some Hurricanes were still taxying from dispersal as the bombs fell close by and were damaged by blast although all but one still took off. Some of the Zeros also kept an eye on the climbing Hurricanes but dutifully remained with the bombers they were protecting.

At the Racecourse No 258 had a few precious minutes' warning. Fighter Operations phoned through to Squadron Leader P. C. Fletcher, the CO, to enquire if anything was known of an enemy force.

'Yes,' said Fletcher, 'they are right overhead and we are taking off now.' So Fighter Operations were being alerted by a squadron, instead of the other way round. The tail was wagging the dog. It was a miserable situation.

By prior arrangement, the tropicalised Mark IIB Hurricanes which had more powerful engines than the desert-weary Mark I's and were 20 m.p.h. faster took off first, led by Fletcher. The IIB's would normally have carried twelve guns, as against the Mark I's eight but, to lighten the aircraft and improve performance, Squadron Leader Fletcher had had four guns removed.

Three minutes later the Mark I's were airborne under Flight Lieutenant 'Denny' Sharp from New Zealand. Sharp was one of the few airmen who had already fought against Japanese planes over Singapore. His exploits have been described by Flying Officer Arthur Donahue, an ex-member of the renowned Eagle Squadron and one of the very first Americans to fly with the RAF. Donahue himself was due to join 258 Squadron just after the Ceylon operations. Before his death over the English Channel towards the end of the year, Donahue was to write *Last Flight from Singapore* (Macmillan), which vividly describes the appalling difficulties under which they operated before the survivors were withdrawn to Palembang.

As 258 Squadron's Hurricanes left the runway, the Japanese were dead overhead, flying inland over Colombo in several loose formations, with the intention of making their attack from the landward side.

The Armed Merchant Cruiser *Hector,* ablaze in Colombo harbour after the Japanese attack.

Pilots of No 258 Squadron (Hurricanes): *Left to Right:* Flight-Lieutenant Peacock-Edwards, unknown, Squadron-Leader Fletcher, Flight-Lieutenant Sharp.

Squadron-Leader Fletcher discusses tactics with his pilots at the Racecourse Aerodrome.

Captain Augustus Agar, VC.

Pilot Officer Charles Gardner.

A Japanese photograph taken as the *Dorsetshire* (background) turns helplessly with her rudder stuck and a salvo of bombs strikes the *Cornwall* (foreground).

Warships in the harbour were the Japanese primary targets. The dive bombers were to look after these. Secondary targets, mainly the concern of Fuchida's Type 97 Attack Bombers, were the Railway Workshops at Ratmalana and the oil depots at Kolonnawa, just east of the City. In the event their bombing was pretty accurate. As they turned in for their bombing runs, six bi-planes were observed far below, strung out in line astern, approaching the city from the north. Fuchida called up Lieutenant Commander Shigeru Itaya from the *Akagi,* who was leading the fighter element, and told him to deal with these. Itaya, another senior man, had himself had a hand in the final design of the Zero as second in command of the Yokasuka Experimental Air Corps in 1938.

The bi-planes were Lieutenant Longsdon's 'Stringbags', which, by a most unhappy stroke of fortune, had arrived over the city at this precise moment, on their way to Ratmalana. Here it was planned that they should refuel and then go forth to attack the enemy fleet.

Regulations required friendly aircraft approaching Colombo to fly in through a recognised corridor from the north at a slow speed and a height of about 2,000 feet. Individual aircraft were to break formation and to fly, spread out in line astern. In a word they were to make clear their friendly intent by putting themselves in a rather vulnerable situation. These rules the six Fleet Air Arm Swordfish meticulously observed. When fighters approached they were not perturbed; the RAF Hurricanes normally came and had a look at aircraft in the lane. Several flew up on a reciprocal course, some 1200 yards away. Sub-Lieutenant Mackay, Longsdon's observer, flashed them 'N', the letter of the day. Leading Airman Skingley, in Sub-Lieutenant Meakin's aircraft, fired the recognition signal (2 green stars). Within a few seconds, to everyone's dismay, the leading fighter, followed at about five second intervals by the other five, turned in to attack. Remarkably accurate fire, from machine guns and cannon, was opened at about 600 yards range.

Handicapped by their torpedoes, the Swordfish took what evasive action they could. There was scarcely time for any sort of defence, but one or two rear gunners were able to bring their guns to bear for a few rounds without any apparent effect on the enemy.

The attackers were now definitely identified as Zero fighters. Most Swordfish received hits in the first attack. Sub-Lieutenant Carter's instrument panel was smashed, his goggles shot off his face and his air gunner, Leading Airman Bolton, badly injured. The attacks were now repeated and within a very few minutes all the Swordfish had been shot down, Carter's into the sea, Sub-Lieutenant Meakin's onto the beach and the others into the paddy fields surrounding the coastal villages. Carter and Bolton were able to abandon their sinking aircraft and make for the shore in their dinghy, though Bolton was to die before reaching dry land.

Not satisfied with having shot down all the planes, the Japanese now came back to gun the wretched survivors. Carter's plane, in the sea, and Meakin's, on the beach, seem to have received the most attention. Though both unhurt in the crash landing, Skingley was killed and Meakin badly injured by these later attentions.

Lieutenant Longsdon himself was badly wounded, 'Half my face was blown off and we ended upside down in a paddy field. A sorry tale.'

Of the 14 men involved, 5 were killed and 5 wounded. One of the pilots lost was Sub-Lieutenant Beale who had been credited with a hit on the *Bismarck* in atrocious conditions in mid-Atlantic.

The six Zeros rejoined the main force which was by then attacking the harbour. To the disappointment of the raiders there was only one obvious British warship in the harbour, the antiquated little destroyer *Tenedos* (Lieutenant R. Dyer) which was undergoing a refit and was immobilised just off one of the jetties. She had been one of the four destroyers escorting the *Prince of Wales* and *Repulse* when they were sunk off Malaya and had brought back as many survivors as could be crowded on her limited deck space.

Though not recognisable as such to the Japanese, there was another vessel serving under the White Ensign as an Armed Merchant Cruiser. She was the *Hector* (Ocean Steamship Co., 11,198 tons) and had for nearly two years been engaged in escorting convoys between the Middle East, India and Australia. She was now in process of being de-commissioned and had only a reduced crew on board, so could not be got to sea.

Also in the harbour, which it is interesting to note Fuchida describes as 'being jammed with cargo vessels', for all the claims made that Colombo had been virtually emptied of ships, was the submarine depot ship *Lucia*.

As it happens these three naval vessels bore the main weight of the Japanese attacks.

The *Lucia* was damaged by bombs, but the other two vessels, the *Tenedos* and *Hector*, received the brunt of the attack and were lost. The *Hector* settled on the bottom to burn steadily for a fortnight. It has been claimed to have been one of the longest marine fires in history. Her derelict hulk remained, a familiar landmark, in the centre of the harbour until raised two years later and beached out of the way a few miles north of the harbour, where her rusting remains can be seen to this day.

A bomb blew off the stern of the *Tenedos,* killing several men. One of these was Ordinary Seaman Sir Robert Peel, Bt., son of Beatrice Lillie, the comedienne. The explosion was made particularly severe by the *Tenedos'* depth-charges detonating and a neighbouring merchantman, the *Benledi,* unloading motor transport and bombs and herself hit by one bomb, was severely damaged by the blast.

By now both squadrons of Hurricanes were taking a hand in the battle. 30 Squadron had been jumped at Ratmalana but several of its pilots engaged the Japanese. Flight Sergeants T. G. Paxton and L. A. Ovens, DFM, put up a splendid fight before they were shot down, Ovens being killed outright and Paxton dying two days later of shock, following multiple burns. In hospital his burns were not considered serious enough to put him on the danger list and he was able to make a full report to his CO and the Squadron Intelligence Officer claiming 'he had engaged and definitely shot down two enemy aircraft. One of these was attacking P/O. Macdonald.'

This was D. A. Macdonald, a Canadian, who force-landed his plane on the Galle Face Green, Colombo's marine promenade. He did so through a hail of ack-ack, sent up by the City's over-enthusiastic gunners. Anxious watchers, uncertain, like the gunners, whether he were friend or foe, were relieved to see him walk into the Colombo Club where he called for a drink. Paxton confirmed that a plane which was Pilot Officer Macdonald's quarry crashed into the sea.

When Paxton was finally attacked and hit the cockpit got so hot that he could no longer hold the throttle and the flames eventually forced him to bail out at only 1,600 feet. He landed in a tree from which he was rescued by some Ceylonese. Unhappily he had left it too late. His burns in the end proved fatal.

It is quite clear that the Japanese had no idea that the Racecourse strip existed. Once Ratmalana had been dealt with they expected the air to be theirs, undisputed. They did not appear to notice 258 Squadron's planes coming up to meet them and it was this squadron which took their toll of the attackers.

Squadron Leader Fletcher recounts how he led the Mark IIB Hurricanes seawards, 'really clawing for height. There was a lot of "lumpy" cloud about, but quite good visibility in between (visibility not so good at sea level). I had clearly seen the tight formation of Jap bombers, with fighters above them, heading rather inland. I deduced they would turn and attack the harbour from the land side.

'We did a climbing turn towards the harbour; I was still hoping against hope to get above them (I thought they were at about 10,000 ft.) but if not, a head-on attack against the formation might be possible. Suddenly a couple of Jap bombers dived down through a gap in the clouds, very close to us. Obviously dive attacks had started. We were still much below the bombers so I had a difficult decision to make. I can remember my thought process very clearly. It looked as if we had not been spotted. There was masses of cloud cover about and if we continued climbing we might get the precious height we needed. On the other hand by that time the bombers would have done a lot of damage; we would be seen by the Zeros sooner or later and would be mixing it with them instead of getting at the bombers.

'I decided to go after the bombers, shouted "Tally-ho" and turned down into a dive through a cloud between us and the gap through which the Japanese were diving. Some of the formation lost me in the cloud, but two or three (and Teddy Peacock-Edwards was one of them) were still with me when we broke cloud and were in a good position to attack.

'From then on it was every man for himself.

'I opened up on one aircraft diving towards the harbour: it partially pulled out but continued straight on and as I did a climbing turn I saw it go into the sea, well outside the harbour.

'I was now pointing inland and remember my anger when I saw that our ack-ack was still firing. I was positioning myself to open up on a bomber pulling up from an attack, had fired a burst which hit the Jap and knocked a few bits off the aircraft, when I felt and heard a heavy thud just below me. I looked quickly around but there were no Zeros near me. It was a burst from our own guns.

'There was more flak, and oil and fumes began to enter the cockpit. I turned towards base and was looking inside to see how serious things were when I felt some cracking bangs into the back of my seat and a twinge of pain in my shoulder.

'There were two Zeros behind me.

'I went into a steep turn, applying full power, at which point oil gushed into the cockpit – quite a bit of it in my face.

'I bailed out with some difficulty, but my troubles were not over. As I was hanging on the end of my parachute two Zeros took it in turns to shoot at me. Half way down, as I heard their guns, I hung limply with my head on one side, pretending to be dead. I do not know if they were deceived but they just flew around me until I landed safely on the edge of a coconut plantation and near a small temple.

'I disentangled myself and saw a Buddhist priest in his yellow robes a few yards away. He had evidently been enjoying a grandstand view. He looked scared; I must have looked a bit frightening because I was covered in oil, my shirt had been ripped off and for some reason I had my revolver in my hand.

'I called to him, in case he thought I was a Japanese. Just at that moment I looked up and saw a Zero beginning a dive at me. We both scuttled into the plantation.

'After a short time the priest found a man with a car who drove me to the Racecourse, from where I was taken to hospital.'

Both Squadron Leader Fletcher and his No. 2 man and fellow Rhodesian, Flight Lieutenant S. R. Peacock-Edwards, were to win the DFC for their part in the battle over Colombo.

Peacock-Edwards, a veteran of the Advanced Air Striking Force which moved into France at the outbreak of war, the Battle of Britain and Malta, describes events thus:

'Our formation commenced to climb in the same direction as the enemy, but sweeping round over the harbour, which was of prime importance, and out to sea. At about 4,000 feet, and just out to sea from the harbour, the enemy, who were by this time just behind and above us, caught up and passed our formation which was still climbing at maximum boost.

'Within a few seconds, however, the enemy broke up and commenced to dive bomb the harbour and shipping off the Galle Face Green. They dived right through our formation which makes me doubt whether they had spotted us. We immediately went in to attack and from then on it was one big dog-fight. I managed to shoot down one Navy 99 into the sea just off the Galle Face Green, but by this time it was every man for himself and the escorting fighters had come down, so I cannot say with any accuracy what happened to the other members of the flight. I was set upon by enemy fighters which I managed to shake off by climbing, but I was followed by two of these and when I found myself in a superior position proceeded to attack the one I considered to be in the most vulnerable position. I followed him down but did not finally observe the results of my attack as I was again set upon by half a dozen fighters.

'This time the position was such that my tactics developed into a game of hide and seek in and around the palm trees. At this altitude the Hurricane was at a distinct disadvantage as opposed to the Navy O. And while four of them held off at a safe height, two continued to carry out head-on and stern attacks on me. I managed to get in some good bursts on the aircraft doing the head-on attacks but the battle was drawing to a close and I observed no definite results. The aircraft was damaged and it is quite possible that it never regained its carrier base.

'The end finally came when I was forced to crash-land in a paddy field. During the impact I must have been dazed because I woke up sitting in a pile of wreckage with an enemy fighter circling overhead. It made no effort to attack until I clambered out of the wreckage, in case fire broke out, and made my way to cover nearby. Hampered by the heavy mud of the paddy field, but with enough time for the fighter to deliver a half-hearted attack on me – fortunately nowhere near – I gained cover. This was a stream at the edge of the field into which I jumped and then made my way to a small road bridge which spanned the stream.'

This is a splendidly typical example of the style in which fighter pilots used to make out their reports once the excitement was over. Years later Teddy Peacock-Edwards would allow us a peep behind the cool phrases. 'There were times,' he says, 'when I was a very frightened young man.'

Clambering out of the stream, he began his return to the Racecourse across a pair of bicycle handlebars. Their owner is always referred to in popular accounts as a 'helpful villager', which is not quite correct. He was in fact a bugler of the Ceylon Light Infantry in mufti, and although Ceylonese (perhaps a Eurasian) went by the unlikely name of McLeod, and happening to be passing by on his bike.

Some of the Fulmars of 803 and 806 Squadrons at Ratmalana gamely took off to join the fray. Four were lost. A Zero shot one down just as it was coming in to land. This two-seater reconnaissance plane had a performance which was little better than that of the Japanese Navy 97 Bomber, which it somewhat resembled. As fighters the Fulmars were not only far slower, but were out-manoeuvred and were literally sitting ducks against Zeros. According to one pilot, 'The only way that we could mix it with the Japs was to dive from a great height out of the sun, have a go and get the hell out of it. These conditions unfortunately were not present on the day of the raid as the Japs already had a 10,000 feet advantage and the Fulmar was a painfully slow climber, even at full boost.'

Admiral Layton was soon to report to the Admiralty, 'Fleet Air Arm aircraft are proving more of an embarrassment than a help, when landed. They cannot operate by day in the presence of Jap fighters and only tend to congest aerodromes.'

It was decided, as soon as results on Easter Sunday had been studied, that the Fulmar could not be used again as a fighting machine against the Japanese. In the event they did have to be used again, as we shall see.

A general breakdown in communications made it very difficult for the authorities to piece together the results of the battle. Even our own air casualties could not be immediately determined with any precision. Squadron Leader Chater at Ratmalana found it necessary to fly to the Racecourse to regain contact and to see if any of his missing Hurricanes were there. Eight had not returned.

Slowly the situation was pieced together.

Pilot Officer Macdonald was safe; his aircraft, much damaged by anti-aircraft fire, being stranded on the Galle Face Green. Pilot Officer Cartwright and Flying Officer Allison had survived crash-landings and were in hospital. Flight Sergeant Paxton was in a serious condition, with severe burns which he did not survive. Only three months before, he had been credited with shooting down a Ju 88 and a Heinkel 111 over the North African desert and the adjacent Mediterranean. Sergeant C. J. Browne was dead. He had been seen to shoot down a bomber but had then been attacked by a Zero and had fallen in flames. Pilot Officers Caswell and Geffene had also been shot down and killed (the latter was American). Flight Sergeant Ovens' aircraft was not located till the 7th when it was found near the Kandy Road. The pilot was dead.

By the evening No 30 Squadron could muster only seven serviceable aircraft. If the Japanese resumed the offensive they would be hopelessly outnumbered.

At the Racecourse 14 Hurricanes had taken off and nine had not returned. Five pilots had been killed (Flight Lieutenants Lockhart and McFadden, Pilot Officers Neill and Tremlett and Sergeant Thain). Squadron Leader Fletcher and Flight Lieutenant Peacock-Edwards, after bailing out, had both suffered injuries and were in hospital.

No 258 Squadron could now muster only 9 aircraft to meet any new attack.

Taking into account the Fleet Air Arm's casualties, we had lost 27 aircraft over Colombo, with seventeen airmen killed and eleven injured.

What of enemy losses?

We claimed 27 enemy planes destroyed. When this figure was announced it caused great rejoicing everywhere. No such claims had yet been made against the Japanese. It was also announced that the enemy had been driven off. This was equally heartening after the succession of depressing communiqués which had emanated from Asia since the Japanese offensive began.

Only three Japanese planes fell on Ceylon soil. One, shot down by Sergeant Browne, fell at Horana, a little south of Ratmalana, one on the playing fields of St. Thomas's College, Mount Lavinia and another at Pitta Kotte, on Colombo's eastern outskirts.

The Japanese admitted the loss of only 5 aircraft, which was probably the figure lost over Colombo itself and the adjacent sea.

Inevitably there must have been those damaged planes which would never have managed the long flight back. Fuchida confirms this. He states that just as he was about to break off the Colombo attack, his radio operator, Petty Officer Mizuki, picked up a radio message transmitted to Admiral Nagumo from one of the cruiser *Tone*'s float-planes, which will be mentioned shortly in this narrative.

This message caused him considerable alarm, for it seemed to indicate that the British Fleet were about to launch a surface attack on the Japanese ships. Since the likely timing of this attack would coincide with the return of his own planes, the carriers' decks would have to be kept clear for them and the launching of planes to take offensive action against the British ships might be badly hampered. It would be some time, too, before his planes could be re-armed with torpedoes or bombs.

His assessment of the situation was unduly pessimistic as it happens, but it led him to order an immediate recall of all the bombers, without waiting to reform. The fighters were left to deal with No 258 Squadron's Hurricanes, which had just appeared on the scene. These fighters thus had to find their own way back to the carriers without the assistance of the bombers' navigators and without the benefit of the homing devices which were fitted only in the bombing planes. He was taking a calculated risk in ordering this. 'Several,' he writes, 'never made it.'

Damage done by the high-level bombers to railway installations was not extensive. Much more effective was the resulting demoralisation of the civilian population, to whom the raid came as a shock, since it had not been considered advisable to issue a prior warning, lest it precipitate a possible panic. The raid had lasted some 20 minutes and civilian casualties amounted to 85 dead and 77 injured. The General Hospital's records show that 47 were treated there. Most of these were from ships and wharves in the harbour where there had been casualties amongst some East African troops unloading food ships.

One unhappy note was struck when bombs (presumably intended for the nearby Kolonnawa oil installations) hit the Mental Hospital at Angoda, killing 7 inmates and injuring many others as well as causing panic and alarm on a tragic scale.

Immediately a huge exodus began from the city. In common with the rest of the world, the Ceylonese had heard of the wholesale massacres of civilians by Japanese troops in China – particularly that at Nanking. Already hideous rumours were in circulation after the fall of Hong Kong and Singapore, where troops had bayoneted both patients and staff at military hospitals and where prisoners of war (many of them Indians) and Chinese civilians (mostly merchants believed hostile to Japan) had been systematically murdered. No Ceylonese wished to share the same experiences. Cars, trains, rickshaws and bullock-carts, packed beyond capacity, put as many miles as possible between them and the prospects of further bombing and possibly invasion. The ferry to India from Talaimannar was packed that night and many nights afterwards.

Under cover of the general confusion the four political detainees at Kandy were able to effect their escape from the prison, of which they were the sole occupants at the time. Naturally enough, they did not lack for sympathisers amongst their countrymen outside the prison, but had managed in addition to enlist the help of one of the prison guards, Solomon by name, a Roman Catholic by religion, although (to quote Dr de Silva) 'it was not usual at that time for Catholics in Ceylon to identify themselves with the LSSP.' Tossing into the yard the key which they had been able to get made so that it would be clear how they had got away, they were quickly picked up by friends outside. Solomon, it seems, went with them.

It was not a difficult matter for the four to drop out of sight of the authorities in Ceylon. Their subsequent activities will be recounted in due course.

The last Zero fighters withdrew from Colombo at about 8.30 a.m. They were seen circling aimlessly just out to see for some 5 minutes waiting no doubt for a rendezvous with the bombers Fuchida had hurriedly sent back. When these did not materialise, they set off to manage as best they could the long flight back to the five carriers. These had already turned away so that the return journey would be rather longer. Admiral Nagumo had held back a second wave of bombers to follow up the initial attack on Colombo if worthwhile targets were found there. It was a big disappointment for him to learn that the British fleet had not been located and that there had been only small pickings for his bombers in the harbour.

He had only just received a signal to this effect when a further message was handed to him. This had originated from a float-plane from the cruiser *Tone* which had been searching the seas to the north-west of the Japanese fleet. It read, 'Two enemy destroyers sighted. Heading south-south-west. Speed 25 knots.' Their position was within range of his remaining bombers. When the float-plane corrected the first signal and proclaimed the two 'destroyers' to be cruisers, Nagumo did not hesitate. He ordered the second bombing force to attack as soon as the Colombo planes had all returned. Meanwhile he ordered the two cruisers to be shadowed.

Led by Lieutenant Commander Takashige Egusa, Air Group Commander of the Soryu, 80 Type 99 Dive-bombers (Vals) took off for the position of the two cruisers at about 11.30 a.m.

Captain Agar in the *Dorsetshire* and Captain P. C. W. Manwaring in the *Cornwall* had detected by radar a second shadowing float-plane on the limits of the horizon. They were not unduly perturbed, however, for they expected to be under the air protection of the *Formidable*'s and *Indomitable*'s planes by 2 p.m. and by their estimates it was unlikely that they were in range of the carrier-borne aircraft with the Japanese fleet. However, both ships' companies took up action stations and they pressed on at maximum speed to rejoin the rest of the Fleet.

It was to be a nasty surprise to learn that the accepted estimate of the range of the Japanese planes was much wide of the mark.

Shortly after 1 o'clock, with all men at action stations, numerous radar contacts were picked up. There was a strong likelihood that they were our own planes but wireless silence was now broken to notify Admiral Somerville of their position, to report the enemy shadowing and the possibility of air attack.

Egusa's pilots had been hand picked as an elite force, trained to destroy America's aircraft-carriers, and had been much dismayed to have found none at Pearl Harbour. They wasted not a moment on sighting the two cruisers but, dividing into two groups, scored hit after hit from the word go. The reports of both Japanese and

British confirm this. The line of attack seems to have been carefully worked out in advance and those manning the anti-aircraft guns were frustrated to find the bombers approaching immediately ahead and retiring astern. Most of the guns were 'blind' on this particular bearing to safeguard the ships' rigging and superstructure.

Young Ray Lock, one of the *Dorsetshire*'s crew serving a Pom-pom gun amidships and fuming at their hopelessly restricted field of fire, found himself flung to the deck 10 feet below by a blast from the first bomb. Shaken, he got to his feet, intent on getting back to the gun, but was startled to see only two blackened stumps where the twin gun barrels had been and the rest of the crew dead or badly wounded. Only some time later, noticing a squelching sound in his shoes, did he find them filling with blood and realised that he was seriously wounded in the chest and legs.

Captain Agar who, when the Allies had attempted vainly to help back 'White' Russians to power after World War I, had earned a VC at Kronstadt, torpedoing a Russian cruiser in a night motor-torpedo-boat attack, has vividly described the *Dorsetshire*'s ordeal. In quick succession bombs struck the aircraft catapult, the wireless telegraph installation near the bridge and the engine and boiler rooms. Her guns blazed away but some were quickly put out of commission by the bombs. The steering jammed hard to starboard, leaving the ship plunging round in a wide circle until all way stopped. Then followed a frightful explosion as a bomb hit one of the magazines. When the valve on the ship's siren was shot away its plaintive wail was added to the confusion and din.

Only eight minutes after the first bomb hit her bows rose above the sea, where by now most of her company were floundering in the hot oily water, and she was gone.

Much the same fate befell the *Cornwall*. During the morning, as the ships made maximum speed towards the rendezvous over a still sea under a blazing sun, the Padre, who was not to survive the day, conducted an Easter Service. It was relayed throughout the ship to all hands as they stood at action stations. As in the *Dorsetshire*, a mid-day meal was brought to the men where they were.

When, at 1.40 p.m., the Jap planes struck, the first bomb hit the *Cornwall*'s port side, astern. The ship shuddered and shook as bomb after bomb went home. She was swung evasively to starboard, which threw her heavily over to port. A.A. gun crews opened fire (and even mistakenly claimed an enemy bomber) but several crews were wiped out.

Lieutenant Geoffrey Grove, her First Lieutenant, relates, 'We watched the planes like hawks, and as the bombs came down we flung ourselves down on our faces. If the hit was close, you found yourself being bounced like a ball. We had three hits almost directly under us and for one of them I was standing up and was enveloped in a great sheet of flame. I thought it was the end of me, but actually my clothing saved me and I was unhurt. Well this couldn't last. We had something like 15 hits in about 7 minutes and the poor old girl took up a bigger list than ever and started to settle. When I could do no more up top, I went below to help put out fires and chuck red hot ammunition into the sea. We got all the fires out quite easily. By now some men were launching the floats. There were some pretty nasty sights around, too harrowing to describe. By this time the ship was obviously sinking, and having got the wounded over the side, we went over the side ourselves. I stepped over a rail (normally 30 feet above sea-level) and slipped quietly into the sea. I had previously blown up my lifebelt and, once clear of the ship turned round and waited for her to go, which she did quite quietly, bows first. Her stern came up into the air and she slid down, one propeller revolving slowly.

'The Japs by this time had formed up in squadrons and flew past in perfect formation, thirty or forty of them, and much to our relief, flew away. We were quite expecting to be machine gunned in the water.'

From both cruisers several whalers and many rafts were left afloat as well as a small motor boat from each ship. Both Captain Manwaring, who had suffered a shoulder injury, and Captain Agar, comparatively unhurt, were fortunate to get away.

The Japanese airmen reported

an all-time record in bombing accuracy. Perhaps the bombing conditions were perfect; whatever the reason, every bomb literally either struck the enemy ships or scored a near miss. So thick were the explosions from the rain of bombs that many plane crews could not determine whether they had actually released their missiles. Only after all our planes had assembled in formation and the pilots could visually check the racks of other planes could we tell whether or not any of the planes were still armed.

Masutake Okumiya, who relates this in *Zero*, adds;

Lieutenant Commander Egusa was my class-mate, both at Etajima (the Japanese Annapolis) and in the Navy Flying School at Kasumigaura. We both were Navy senior dive-bomber pilots. Shortly after the Indian Ocean operation . . . I asked my old friend how his planes had sunk the British warships.

'Egusa looked at me and shrugged. "It was much simpler than bombing the *Settsu*. That's all."
'The *Settsu*! Simpler than bombing Japan's old target battleship!'
Thus, in a few minutes, Japanese naval airmen had demonstrated that their dive-bombers could be just as effective against ships at sea as the land-based, high-level and torpedo bombers of the Saigon-based Air Corps who had sunk the *Prince of Wales* and *Repulse*.
We now had to acknowledge them masters of all three techniques.
Japanese successes for the day were not yet over. It will be remembered that the morning had started for Admiral Somerville with the receipt in the *Warspite* of a series of disturbing distress signals from merchant ships. Most of these had been sent off by six ships forming a somewhat loose, straggling convoy which was hugging the coast on a southerly course in the area of Vizagapatam. None of these ships survived the day. They were the *Autolycus* (whose fate is described later in some detail), the *Indora*, the *Malda*, the *Exmoor*, the *Silksworth* and the *Shinkuang*.
During the afternoon two aircraft from the *Ryujo*, the carrier in Admiral Ozawa's Malaya Force, had found another target south-east of Vizagapatam. The merchant ship *Dardanus*, still following the coastal route southwards, was hit by bombs in the

engine room and brought to a stop. A second attack by the two planes as the ships boats got away scored hits. However, Captain English and others of the ship's company decided to return to the ship once the aircraft had departed and pumps were got working and holes temporarily plugged.

The British India Company's steamer *Gandara* now arrived on the scene and gallantly took the stricken *Dardanus* in tow towards Madras. When night fell the two ships were making steady headway and the prospect of salvaging the Dardanus began to look good.

*

As the sun set on the whole theatre of operations that Easter Sunday evening there seemed at last some prospect of a few hours respite, at least, from the general tension.

Much of Colombo's population continued to stream out of the city.

Ground crews at Ratmalana and the Racecourse strove feverishly to get the remaining Hurricanes into a serviceable state. Many of the experienced flyers were now dead or out of action. The small band of survivors prepared for the next attack. They were to be up again at 4 a.m. and on immediate readiness at daybreak.

Hospital staffs, both civil and military, were working at full pressure. Funeral arrangements were being made for the dead.

The *Hector* blazed still, in the middle of the Harbour.

The survivors from the lost Catalina began their second night, crammed into the dark purgatory of their paint locker in the *Isokaze*.

That evening from Radio Ceylon, the Governor, Sir Andrew Caldecott, made a broadcast praising the civil population for their courage and calmness, which sentiments were largely countermanded in a subsequent broadcast.

And 400 miles out at sea, nearly a thousand sailors, in two groups, prepared for a night in the water, their ships fathoms deep below them with many of their shipmates. 'I told them,' says Captain Agar, 'we would have to stick it out, whatever happened; for I was certain help would come. The British Navy never leaves its comrades in the lurch.'

Though there were many survivors of the 'Forlorn Battle' of the Java Seas who might have told them differently, his confidence was fortunately not to be misplaced.

CHAPTER SEVEN

Hide and Seek

'God was with us . . . otherwise we could not possibly
have got away with it.'
PILOT OFFICER CHARLES GARDNER

So far this narrative must inevitably give the impression of a certain
defeatism in the British camp, with no countermeasures being
planned against the Japanese Fleet, now extended so far from their
home bases that they would have had the greatest trouble in getting
back any lame ducks, damaged in action.

In fact from the moment the presence of the enemy fleet had been
suspected no one had lost sight of the need to strike back. The main
weapon at hand, of course, was the Eastern Fleet. If surface vessels
were not to be brought into action, the carriers, *Formidable* and
Indomitable, each had a squadron of Swordfish or Albacores, though
it is now difficult to see these slow, old bi-planes, which would have
been hopelessly outnumbered by the Zero fighters which would
have gone up to meet them, constituting a serious threat to the
Japanese. Furthermore, we now know that, in order to bring enemy
ships within the Swordfish's rather limited range, our carriers
would have had to steam in for 50 or 60 miles, at the least, within
the perimeter of the Japanese Dive Bombers' effective range before
our own planes could be launched, where they would have been
subject to attack for the whole distance. Night operations from
carriers then, as now, presented enormous difficulties and risks but
they were contemplated. To Admiral Somerville this seemed our
only hope.

We have seen how, within 12 hours of Birchall's sighting report
being received, six Swordfish aircraft of No 788 Squadron had
moved immediately to Ratmalana to strike at the enemy from a
land base, which could reasonably have been carried out at night.
By the greatest ill luck they had been lost.

Though the medium bomber is far less useful against ships than the torpedo bomber, this left only the single RAF Squadron, No 11, with Blenheims, available to strike back at Admiral Nagumo's Air Striking Force. When they moved to the Racecourse just over a week before the Japanese threat developed they had fortuitously saved themselves from likely destruction on the ground, for Fuchida's planes would certainly have spotted them at Ratmalana. This they failed to do at the Racecourse.

When, at about 7.45 on Sunday morning, the huge flight of Japanese aircraft came roaring over Colombo, Wing Commander A. J. M. Smyth, DFC, was preparing to lead ten Blenheims, with 500 lb. semi-armour-piercing bombs, to seek out the enemy fleet, using Bradshaw's sighting point from which to calculate the fleet's likely position. With 258's Hurricanes monopolising the runway, and so many enemy fighters overhead, a take-off was out of the question for the duration of the raid, but at 8.30 they were off.

One returned with engine trouble. The others pressed on.

Nagumo had turned westwards after launching the Colombo raid, and had continued on that course to assist Egusa's planes, seeking out the *Dorsetshire* and *Cornwall*. The Blenheims flew southwards, on the assumption that the Japanese would have turned southwards from the point where Flight Lieutenant Bradshaw's Catalina had sighted them earlier that morning. Wing Commander Smyth must have flown too far East, for he missed the Fleet altogether and returned to Colombo at 14.30, their mission unfulfilled. The range of the Blenheim did not allow them to do much of a search.

Though the chances were slender of 11 Squadron doing any serious damage to the Japanese ships without being wiped out themselves, their failure to locate the enemy was a pity. For after sending back their invaluable sighting report early in the day, Bradshaw and his crew in their Catalina, using the most skilful tactics, had been doing a splendid job keeping an eye on the warships for most of the day, and the fact that they managed this and returned safely to Koggala was one of the major triumphs of the day.

Pilot Officer Charles Gardner, Bradshaw's second pilot, relates how this was done. 'God was with us because the carrier force aircraft were all away; otherwise, in the clear blue sky, we could not possibly have got away with it. As it was we were, of course, seen and were shot at by a battleship's main armament – two or three salvoes – all of which splashed into the sea behind us. We returned to Dondra Head, the southern tip of Ceylon, which provided a useful navigational check on the Japanese Fleet's exact position, and from there we sent off a full amplifying report.

'We then shadowed this Fleet for the rest of the day. We invented on the spur of the moment an obvious tactic for survival. We flew at wave-slapping height and then, with all the crew placed at vantage points for look out, pulled briefly up to 100 feet. If no Japanese masts broke the horizon we went down to nought feet again and flew on to where the distant horizon had been. Here we repeated the exercise. In this way we successfully shadowed the Japanese, never, after the initial identification, seeing more than the tops of their masts and never even being identified as a radar blip to them. (We did not know then that the enemy ships were not equipped with radar). We did not see the Japanese aircraft return nor, mercifully, did we see any Japanese aircraft at all.'

Even before they landed Flight Sergeant Redmond took off and, later that night, Flying Officer Round. Both flew long searches but did not sight the Japanese Fleet.

No 11 Squadron's Blenheims carried out a second sweep on the 7th, but by then Nagumo was miles to the south, turning eastwards, out of range of all reconnaissance. He had sailed on a course to put the maximum distance between his fleet and Ceylon until that morning, when he turned north-eastwards again.

We were now completely in the dark as to Japanese movements. No one doubted, however, that Nagumo would strike again.

On receiving Birchall's sighting report on the 4th evening, Admiral Somerville had, somewhat impulsively, moved eastwards with those of his ships which were ready to move – the comparatively small Force A. It is difficult to say what his motives were. If they were aggressive the report of the attack on Colombo early on the 5th, particularly in the matter of its great strength, confirmed in every particular the garbled signal received from Birchall's Catalina the previous evening. Somerville realised now that it would be madness to entertain any such idea. He had learnt too of the presence of Ozawa's second fleet in the Bay of Bengal, whose composition was not yet known. The whole picture indicated an impending invasion of Ceylon, aimed at India in conjunction with the drive through Burma. At such a moment a defeat would so damage Allied prospects, that Admiral Somerville was compelled to consider the preservation of his Fleet as his primary object.

Mindful of Sir Dudley Pound's admonition, he turned away and rejoined the rest of the Fleet. To divide it in the circumstances may have been unwise. His two carriers and his few Swordfish aircraft, against five enemy carriers with their much more up to date air component, now known to be extremely efficient, could look forward only to disaster.

Considering the thoroughness of the Japanese air reconnaissance (practically nothing was left afloat on the entire length of the sea route from Calcutta past Madras and round Ceylon to Colombo) and bearing in mind that Nagumo's express orders were to find and destroy the British Fleet, it is astonishing that, regardless of whether he wished it or not, Admiral Somerville's main force was never located by the Japanese.

The author of a book, *Admiral of the Pacific, the Life of Yamamoto*,[1] John Deane Potter, writes:

> For the next three days the five Japanese carriers, with their escorting battleships and cruisers, sailed around, deliberately letting themselves be seen by the RAF reconnaissance planes. By this method Nagumo hoped to entice Somerville's fleet into a decisive daylight battle. Somerville refused to fall into the trap. If he engaged in a daylight battle, hundreds of Japanese planes would pound his ships into the Indian Ocean. He wanted what the Japanese also often tried to achieve – a night surface action.

Other accounts give the impression that Admiral Somerville was fervently but fruitlessly searching for the Japanese Fleet. But neither version accords with the facts.

When he found no major fleet units at Colombo, Nagumo could only assume that they were at Trincomalee or that they had put to sea on receipt of Birchall's signal. This would place them within, at

[1] Heinemann

the most, 100 to 150 miles of Ceylon and this area was strenuously searched by his reconnaissance planes. It is likely that the south-westerly course on which the *Dorsetshire* and *Cornwall* were sailing when they were sunk may have been interpreted as headlong retirement. If the Japanese had only thought to have investigated more closely the reason for this course and had protracted it they would inevitably have come upon the ships they were seeking. But Nagumo, even before Egusa's bombers had been recovered, began a withdrawal to the South-east and, keeping at a respectable distance, made a wide, skirting movement of Ceylon. The one direction in which he does not seem to have thought of searching was to the west and south-west. Such Japanese accounts as have survived mention being sighted by British aircraft on only two occasions – by Birchall, and by a second Catalina, as will be seen later.

The fact is that Addu Atoll, with all its shortcomings, had proved a blessing indeed. It had been the saving of the British Eastern Fleet (or most of it) from destruction.

Before Nagumo struck his next blow, it is worth following Admiral Ozawa's operations along India's eastern seaboard.

We left the *Dardanus* being towed shorewards by the *Gandara* as Sunday night fell. Hopes were high that she might be saved. But they were on a recognised sea route and the Japanese had the route under close surveillance.

Early on the following morning a Jap flying boat arrived on the scene. It seems to have been a standard practice to carry a small bomb load on reconnaissance flights and the Gandara and her tow were easy meat. Both ships replied with their limited armament but the airmen were not deterred. However, when their bombs had been expended the two ships were still afloat and still under way. The Japanese flyers called up surface forces to complete the job. Three cruisers appeared at high speed and held the two helpless merchantmen in a remorseless fire. The *Gandara* had perforce to slip her tow, but even now both ships remained afloat. Yet another Japanese warship ultimately appeared, a light cruiser this time, which finished the two off, at first with shellfire and, when this did not have the desired effect, with torpedoes.

Happily the *Dardanus*'s boats reached the shore on the 7th and surprisingly enough, after their ordeal, none of her exhausted crew were missing. After the gallant assistance they had afforded the stricken *Dardanus* the *Gandara*'s crew deserved well. They did, however, lose a few men.

The flying boat which had sighted the *Dardanus* had taken off just before dawn from the Andamans, where there was a passable anchorage at Port Blair. A second Japanese plane, described as a sea-plane, and no doubt a spotter aircraft launched from one of the cruisers, began its patrol about 150 miles north of the flying-boat's search area and found a likely target at much the same time.

This was the *Autolycus,* still on its way south from Calcutta. Captain Neville had been advised, before leaving Calcutta, that there was quite a large fleet in the vicinity; his informant, a Naval Control Service Officer, seems not to have made it clear that this was a hostile fleet and Captain Neville was under the impression that it was friendly.

Spotters on the *Autolycus* can therefore be congratulated when they identified the sea-plane as hostile and opened fire on it. One must repress the uncharitable thought that they would have done the same had the plane been British! It is not very likely that they would have known that there were no friendly sea-planes (as opposed to flying-boats) in this theatre of war.

When warships appeared from astern Captain Neville was relieved. A salvo of heavy shells swiftly disillusioned him. The ships were Japanese and shells fell steadily and accurately on the luckless *Autolycus.* The ship had to be abandoned, and although most of the crew reached the coast of Orissa, sixteen lives were lost.

There were many such incidents during the week, of which the world heard little. On the east coast the surface raiders' toll was 23 ships, totalling 112,000 tons. Submarines, mainly on the west coast, added 5 more to bring the total to 144,000 tons. The sinkings were unexpected and anger was felt amongst merchant seamen that no protection of any sort seemed available, either on the surface or from the air.

With all this activity off the coast and with the news of the Colombo attack now generally released, it seemed probable that a similar raid on Madras would develop and an air raid warning was sounded on the 7th. Immediately there was a rapid exodus from Madras as there had been from Colombo, though no planes, in the event, approached the city or harbour.

Though the news of the Japanese attack on Colombo was to have this unfortunate consequence in Madras, to the rest of the world the facts, as presented by British communiqués, came as a most welcome and heartening surprise. As a matter of policy the loss of warships was never reported at the time. Such information was often of too much assistance to the enemy who might be uncertain of the final results of an attack. Our losses in warships were not announced until much later and were not then connected with the Japanese sortie. Merchant ship losses were not announced at all. What was announced was a large scale air attack on Colombo, with indifferent results and heavy losses inflicted on the enemy. Furthermore it was implied that this was an invasion force (which the authorities for some time believed to be the case), that they had failed to secure air superiority and had withdrawn.

A great deal of skill and equivocation went into the wording of communiqués during the war, and both sides exercised their ingenuity to the full in framing them. Bombers were said to have been 'driven off' or to 'have dropped their bombs and fled' as though it was an ignoble action not to fly around the target area for a while and allow the defences to take pot shots at them.

At all events there was enormous elation in the Allied camp, and spirits rallied everywhere.

The news was opportune.

In London General Marshall and Mr. Harry Hopkins, President Roosevelt's personal emissary, arrived by air on the 7th evening to concert future Allied plans against the Axis powers and it must have been welcome news to hear that for once a Japanese attack had been repulsed.

However, whatever the communiqués might say, the Chiefs of Staff Committee were under no illusions as to the seriousness of the situation, and in India reports from Ceylon arrived too late to save the Cripps Mission from failure. In any event, any pleasure the news might have given was tempered by the general apprehension, in Madras as well as elsewhere, that more was to come.

A few light bombs were actually dropped on Indian soil on the 6th. These fell at Cocinada and Vizagapatam, doing no significant damage; but they were enough to empty both towns. The appearance of boatloads of survivors elsewhere along the coast alerted many others to the imminence of the Japanese. Things were not helped when the Governor of Madras, Sir Arthur Hope, issued a general warning that invasion might be imminent. Government departments began a planned evacuation programme. Troops even began 'immobilising operations' in the port and dislocating rail tracks. Tension quickly spread throughout southern India. In such an atmosphere there was no room for satisfaction at the RAF's modest triumphs over Colombo.

Better situated now that all the units of the Eastern Fleet had been re-united, Admiral Somerville had stood clear of Addu Atoll in case the Japanese made an offensive move there. When nothing happened, he realised that the pressure had been relaxed. All contacts had been lost with the Japanese who were, in fact, heading well clear of the area at full speed. It was now safe to move north-eastwards to the aid of the two cruisers' survivors.

On the afternoon of the 5th, only two hours after the sinkings, a Swordfish had located them, floating amidst the oil and debris, and a destroyer had been despatched to the scene. But she had been recalled when it seemed likely that the Japanese were approaching the vicinity. Though heartened to have been located, it was bitterly disappointing for the shipwrecked men when night fell with no signs of rescue.

By mid-day on the 6th the rescue of the survivors became Somerville's main concern.

The night had gone painfully slowly for the men in the water. Someone would call out 'What's the time?', for several wrist watches kept going through it all. Everyone would mentally guess the answer ('At least four o'clock'), but it would prove not to be much after eleven.

There had inevitably been a few deaths; mainly those who had been injured in the bombing. Their bodies were kept within the group lest sharks be attracted. Quite a few of these were seen, though there is no recorded instance of an attack. Three out of the *Dorsetshire*'s four surgeons had been casualties but everything was done for the wounded that was possible in the circumstances. They were gathered in and laid in the boats; A. B. Lock was one of them. To a man with severe burns or mutilations the combination of salt water and fuel oil, at first uncomfortably hot, could only exacerbate the pain.

'The wounded men were worrying us a good deal,' reports Lieutenant Grove, chest deep in water with several others in an overcrowded float, 'they would die if we couldn't get them out of the water soon, and so we decided to try and join up with the motor boat, where we hoped there might be a doctor. It took us two hours to pull that quarter of a mile. The Major (Trailen), myself, a stoker and a seaman called Galbraith, who was a survivor from the *Prince of Wales,* took it in turns and I must say at times we thought it would never come any closer. However we reached it in the end and managed to get the wounded in. Poor blokes, they cursed us for clumsy bastards as we had to hurt them like hell to get them there, but you can imagine the difficulties of shifting a heavy man out of a low lying float into a boat when he and you and the boat and the float are slippery with fuel oil.'

Throughout the night, though out of sight of each other, the two groups of survivors had occasionally heard each other, for the sea remained calm and the night air was still. In spite of their nearness to the equator it became rather cold.

And the hours passed unbelievably slowly.

But at last the sun broke the horizon again. It cheered them at first and its warmth was very welcome to the shivering men. Spirits rose for with the dawn rescue would surely come. There was even much laughter amongst the *Dorsetshire*'s company when the Bosun piped hands to breakfast. Salvaged oranges and canteen dripping seem to have been their fare. For each of the *Cornwall*'s men it was a tiny piece of corned beef, followed by tinned apricots, punctured first of all and passed round for a swig at the juice, then opened up and an apricot distributed all round. The various boats also had intact their emergency rations of water, ship's biscuit and tinned milk, most of which went to the wounded.

When the sun rose higher and there were no signs of rescue, the temporary elation began to wane. As is not always realised, perhaps the greatest danger and hardship, adrift at sea in tropical waters, is from the sun. Day long exposure to its rays produces the severest sunstroke and may even cause death. This was appreciated and heads were kept covered with whatever articles of clothing could be found.

Amongst the survivors, tucked away in somebody's shirt, was a small kitten which had been found floundering in the oily water and would live, like many of its more fortunate shipmates, to tell the tale.

Throughout the day there were successive cries announcing a ship on the horizon, raising everyone's hopes, only to have them dashed again. But at last, at about 5 p.m., when they had all been in the water for over 26 hours, an aircraft appeared and signalled, 'Hold on. Help coming.'

With little time left before darkness, at about 6 p.m., the cruiser *Enterprise* and the destroyers *Paladin* and *Panther* arrived on the scene and the survivors' ordeal was over.

'So what do you think we did?' asks Geoffrey Grove. 'Turned to and finished up the apricots!'

After radio silence had been broken on the previous day, before the sinkings, the two cruisers' position was known to the fleet. In any event their course and speed as they pressed on to the appointed rendezvous could be accurately calculated. Fortunately for the survivors there must have been time during the attacks for hasty signals to be despatched, for it was common knowledge in the other ships as early as mid-afternoon on Sunday that the *Dorsetshire* and *Cornwall* were lost.

Enterprise, Paladin and *Panther* were detailed to pick up survivors that very afternoon and immediately parted company with *Warspite* and the faster element of the fleet. On the basis of the planned rendezvous scheduled for Sunday afternoon at about 5 p.m. this should have meant a mere four hours steaming to the site of the sinkings; in fact they took twenty four, including twelve hours in daylight on the 6th. It is likely that they were ordered by Somerville to hold off until Japanese movements were more clearly understood.

As Monday afternoon drew on Captain Annesley in the *Enterprise* warned the ship's company that the search would have to be called off soon after nightfall. This was worrying for young A. B. Duncan

('Jock') Kennedy who knew that the Regulation Petty Officer in the *Cornwall,* George Mariner, was engaged to marry his widowed mother in Cape Town. He was therefore as relieved as anyone when the cry went up from the mast-head crow's nest look-out that a large group of men had been sighted in the water.

Boats were soon lowered and the collection of men from the water went on until after dark, with faint lights being shown by the rescuing ships. For the risk of attack by submarine was great. Throughout all these operations the fleet was much concerned over this possibility for they were apprised from time to time of attacks on merchant ships being carried out in these very waters.

The worst injured soon found themselves in comfortable sick-bays. Sadly enough, in spite of expert medical attention, death now claimed many who had survived, not only their wounds, but the ordeal in the sea. Kennedy estimates that between twenty and thirty were buried at sea from the *Enterprise* over the next few days. His mother was never to see her fiancé again. His anxious enquiries had by now made his fate clear. Suffering from wounds which he knew must be fatal, Petty Officer Mariner had encouraged others to leave the *Cornwall* and had then gone down with the ship.

While the *Cornwall*'s men were taken on board the *Enterprise,* the survivors from the *Dorsetshire* were shared between the two destroyers. Commander Pugsley, RAN, of the *Paladin* was Captain Agar's host for the return to Addu Atoll. Here a supply ship was converted to a temporary hospital ship for the many casualties.

Out of a total complement of 1,546 officers and men in the two cruisers, 1,122 survivors were eventually counted.

These figures could so easily have been much worse.

Apprised of the facts, it seems by Admiral Layton from Colombo, an anxious Admiralty sent definite instructions on the following day, the 7th April, that the Eastern Fleet was not to return to Ceylon harbours. They went further and ordered the withdrawal to East Africa of the slow, out-gunned battleships, *Ramillies, Resolution, Royal Sovereign* and *Revenge.*

On one point we were all agreed [writes Churchill,] the R's should get out of danger at the earliest moment. When I put this to the First Sea Lord there was no need for argument. Orders were sent accordingly.

Admiral Willis prepared for their departure westwards with an escort of destroyers. With them would go the survivors from *Dorsetshire* and *Cornwall*. In the event they steamed out of Addu Atoll early on the 9th. On the same day the faster element 'Force A' also left for Bombay. Only a few auxiliaries and supply ships now remained in the anchorage.

Once again we were concerned to keep track of the Japanese warships. Where had they gone?

It was unlikely that we had seen the last of them. No one seems to have considered this a possibility. The most informed observers were still thinking in terms of invasion. Perhaps of Ceylon only; or of southern India as well.

In Ceylon, the depleted Hurricane and Fulmar squadrons continued to stand by, steeling themselves each day for the enemy's next visitation.

Monday, Tuesday and even Wednesday went by with no new attack, but on Wednesday afternoon a Catalina of 240 Squadron, flown by Flying Officer Round, probing far out to the east at extended range, sighted the enemy again and cleared up the mystery of their whereabouts and likely intentions. An enemy fighter approached the flying boat but mercifully there was cloud cover available. Round disappeared into this, was recalled, and returned safely to Koggala late that night . . .

Vice-Admiral Nagumo had stood well clear of the island and had spent two days refuelling and preparing for a further assault. He had much to congratulate himself for and his ships were unscathed. But he had still not carried out his primary task of destroying the British fleet and gaining undisputed control of the Indian Ocean.

At approximately this time an ancient native sailing craft, the *Sederhana Djohanis,* with 16 British officers, a Malay and a Chinese on board (including an old school friend of the author's – Udney Lind) sailed unsuspectingly into the theatre of operations. After escaping from Singapore they had commandeered the vessel at Padang in Sumatra and had spent many days at sea, making slow progress westwards.

On one occasion they had been sighted and half-heartedly gunned by a plane bearing Japanese markings, but at this stage they believed they were approaching friendly waters and were looking forward to an early end to their ordeal. Once again a plane approached them and when this was also seen to be Japanese their feelings can be imagined. Furthermore, they now sighted two tankers, also Japanese, heading eastwards.

Surprised and dismayed, they could only conclude that Ceylon had already gone the way of Malaya and the Dutch East Indies.

This particular party was to be more fortunate than others, for at least one craft is known to have been waylaid by Japanese fleet auxiliaries and the escapees on board to have been made prisoner.

On the morning of the 6th, just before 10 o'clock, one of the numerous Japanese planes carrying out wide patrols throughout the area sighted the merchant ship *Anglo-Canadian* and attacked her. A fire was started and some slight damage done, but this was quickly brought under control. This ship would in due course play a part in the rescue of the party on board the *Sederhana Djohanis*.

On the afternoon of the 7th, the six 413 Squadron prisoners were at last freed from the paint locker in the *Isokaze*. They were transferred to the flagship, the aircraft-carrier *Akagi,* where the injured then received medical attention which Sergeant Catlin, the Flight Engineer, thought 'the best possible'. For the others conditions remained hardly less conventional than before. Their new accommodation consisted of an aircraft repair well at the bottom of which a tarpaulin had been laid down. They were given blankets and pillows. Here they were kept under strong lights, day and night.

When sighted by Flying Officer Round on the Wednesday afternoon, some 500 miles east-south-east of Ceylon, the Japanese Fleet were heading at full speed on a north-westerly course. It did not take much thought to divine their intentions.

This time their objective was Trincomalee.

CHAPTER EIGHT

Nagumo Follows Up

'We were now on fire from end to end, and sinking. Still
the Japanese planes came on.'
LIEUTENANT DENNIS BRIMBLE,
HMS HERMES

Trincomalee, unlike Colombo, has even now no large urban
population. In 1942, apart from the dockyard area, it was little
more than a large scattered village, with a population
predominantly Tamil, for the climate is less inviting here than on
the west coast where there is heavier rainfall and the land is more
fertile. Clustered about the various bays and inlets in the harbour
itself and in Koddiar Bay there were numerous fishing villages, but
it was unlikely that, if bombers attacked, they would disturb these
or would cause civilian casualties of any significance in
Trincomalee itself.

On the 8th afternoon, as soon as the new sighting of the Japanese
Fleet became known, the decision was taken to clear the harbour as
far as possible. The most important of the few ships at anchor was
the aircraft carrier *Hermes* (Captain Richard Onslow) which had
arrived there on the 4th after parting company with the main fleet.
Only one warship was to remain in the harbour throughout the
emergency. This was the old monitor *Erebus,* launched in 1916, and
a mere platform for a large 15 inch gun. She was of no use in the
present situation. The veteran Australian destroyer *Vampire*
(Lieutenant Commander W. T. A. Moran RAN) was in company
with the *Hermes.* A tanker, the *British Sergeant,* had been discharging
fuel at China Bay. The Fleet Auxiliary *Athelstane,* the cable ship
Hecla and a new Flower Class corvette, the *Hollyhock,* also lay at
anchor in the huge, natural deep-water harbour, as well as a single
merchantman, the *Sagaing* (she of the alleged cargo of whiskey,
though the records talk of 'general and military cargo' which
included a Walrus and 3 Albacore aircraft as deck cargo).

The latter vessel was immobilised, as was the *Erebus*. But at about 4 p.m. the others were ordered to move out and disperse.

In the *Hermes* the recall signal was immediately hoisted and every measure was adopted to spread the order ashore; but in spite of the smallness of the town and the few available entertainments at Trinco, the signal was not immediately seen by everyone. It was 7 p.m, before she weighed anchor and darkness fell as she made for the open sea. With her went the *Vampire*. The *Athelstane* and *Hollyhock* also left together and the *British Sergeant* sailed alone. These fanned out and it was hoped they would be able to disappear from the Japanese view. If as much had been known then as later of the thoroughness of Japanese aerial reconnaissance it would have served better to leave the ships where they were.

For the past few months the *Hermes* had carried out regular patrols between Simonstown, Mombasa, Mauritius, the Persian Gulf and the Maldive Islands. She had been scheduled to move to Australia to help in her defence if the Japanese moved southwards, but by now it had been settled that she would take part in the Madagascar operations due to begin in the following month. Except for two Swordfish under repair in her hangars all her planes were left at China Bay. The old ship was thus extremely vulnerable to air attack, if spotted. Her sole aim was to get clear of trouble. She set off southwards, keeping well clear of the coast. If she could place sufficient distance between herself and Trincomalee, she would be well out of the Japanese line of approach and would quite likely be missed. The other ships fanned out as soon as they had rounded Foul Point and were clear of Koddiar Bay.

In *Hermes* soon after the middle watch the ship's company was called to action stations. Over the broadcasting system came warnings to keep anti-flash gear, life-jackets and all the paraphernalia of battle close to hand. She still steamed hard southwards.

In the Japanese carriers all was activity again. Take-off was scheduled for sunrise. It was the formula as before, but this time they would find the fleet. This would be a second Pearl Harbour, with the British Eastern Fleet the victims. In one particular, and one particular only, did the arrangements differ from those made at Pearl Harbour and Colombo.

It was not a Sunday morning.

Quite unaware that they had been sighted again, Admiral Nagumo hoped to achieve surprise. In fact, as the darkness began to lighten, yet another flying boat, moving in carefully, was seeking them out. At 2.30 a.m., Flight Lieutenant 'Tommy' Thomas, who had flown out General Nye to Cairo, took up the shadowing duties in 'Y for Yorker'. This Catalina he had ferried across the Atlantic and flown ever since. They climbed into the night sky from Koggala lagoon and headed east.

Before daylight *Hermes*' four Bofors guns were manned as well as her Oerlikons and the two 4 inch guns on her stern. Her main 5.5 inch armament was below the flight deck, so could not be elevated against aircraft.

Over on the west coast, No 11 Squadron was alerted for an attack on the enemy fleet as soon as it could be located within range. They would be led this time by Squadron Leader K. Ault, the senior flight commander. Thomas's report was therefore anxiously awaited.

Sure enough, at 7 a.m., soon after darkness had lifted, his first message began to come in. It was however the Emergency Signal. This suddenly broke off and contact could not be regained.

The fighters at China Bay thus received all the warning they needed. No one had any shadow of a doubt that the Colombo attack was to be repeated against Trincomalee and China Bay.

Save in this matter of adequate warning, the events of the 9th April were to bear a quite extraordinary resemblance to the previous Sunday's. The stage was thus set for Ceylon's second trial of strength with the Japanese.

At about 6.20 a.m., when the sun's rays began to lighten up the sky behind the speeding carriers, Fuchida again took off, leading a force consisting of 91 bombers and 38 fighters, substantially the same force as had attacked Colombo on the previous Sunday. The fleet was spread over more than 15 square miles of sea, and the thunder of aero engines must have been audible for a great distance.

261 Squadron's Hurricanes, under Squadron Leader A. G. Lewis, DFC, had been standing tensely by since before dawn on the 5th and had flown patrols and been scrambled on several occasions since then on what had proved to be false alarms. A useful satellite

The last moments of the *Cornwall*.

Cornwall survivors, after 28 hours in the sea await rescue by HMS *Enterprise*.

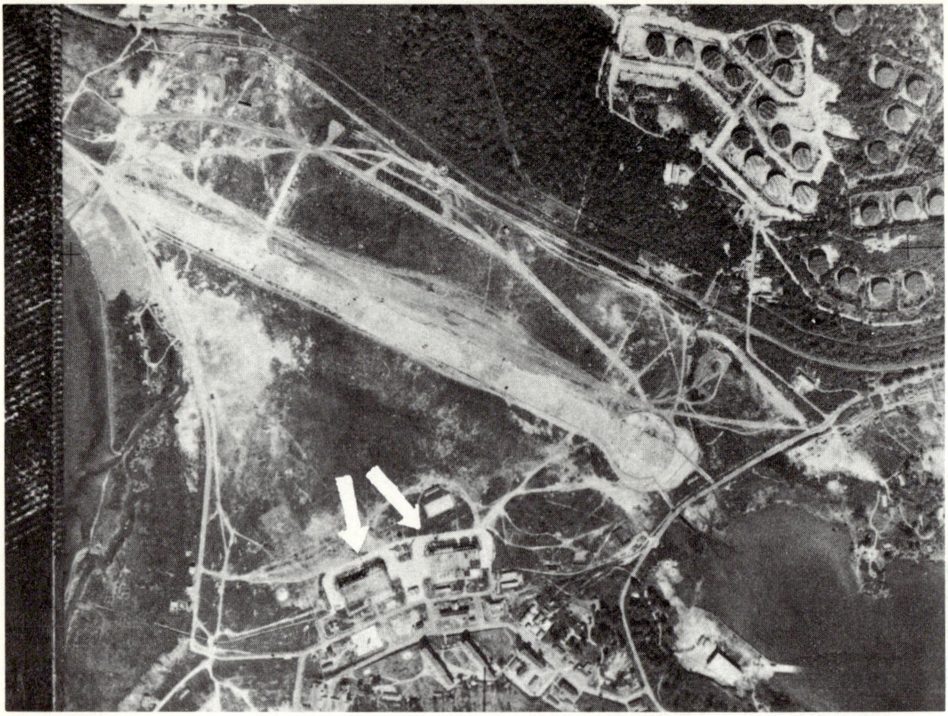

China Bay aerodrome. The two hangars (arrowed) are still roofless after the Japanese raid. Naval oil tanks are visible in the top right-hand corner.

RAF Station, China Bay, taken from above Tambalagam Bay. Beyond is Trincomalee Harbour and the open sea.

Flying Officer Rae ('Tommy') Thomas.

Squadron-Leader Ault leads his formation of Blenheims over Colombo. Five did not return from the attack on the Japanese Fleet.

Found in the jungle near Ceylon's East Coast two years after the Japanese raid, the remains of one of the missing Fulmars.

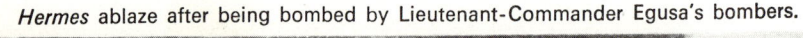

SS *Sadaing* burnt out and beached in the shallows of Trincomalee Harbour.

Hermes ablaze after being bombed by Lieutenant-Commander Egusa's bombers.

strip near the coast at Kokkilai, some 15 miles north of Trincomalee, had been prepared and a Flight was kept there during daylight hours. Here they were unlikely to be spotted. The strip was barely long enough and one precious Hurricane had been written off on the 6th when a sergeant pilot had overshot and crashed into some trees.

At China Bay there had been two mishaps. On the 5th a warrant officer had taxied his Hurricane into a ditch and damaged the port wheel and airscrew and on the 7th a sergeant had crashed on landing. But the worst accident of all was at Kokkilai on the same day. An old Seal amphibious bi-plane, borrowed from 273 Squadron, with two 261 Squadron pilots on board and the squadron medical officer, struck a stationary Swordfish on take-off. All three were killed. On the 8th as many of the squadron as could be spared from constant stand-by made the mournful journey round the harbour into Trincomalee for the triple funeral.

With three Hurricanes and two pilots lost from accidents within the space of three days, just when they were to be most needed, it was a miserable prelude for the message that greeted them on their return. The Japanese were once again within striking range of Ceylon.

On the Thursday a dawn patrol of three Hurricanes was off and into the air as early as 6.35 a.m. Strong radar contacts now began to come in from the east. Six more fighters, led by Flight Lieutenant Cleaver, were off by 7.10 and five minutes later another six, under Flight Lieutenant Marshall, were scrambled from Kokkilai. Squadron Leader Lewis took off rather later.

Six Fulmars of No 273 Squadron, though their chances against the Zero were slender, also gamely took off to join the fray.

So this time fighters were in the air to meet the raiders. Fuchida reports 'Enemy radar must have detected our approach, for Hurricane fighters came out to intercept before we reached the target'.

The three defending fighter sections strove to get at the bombers, but were compelled to engage in dog-fights with the Zeros. The battle raged at a great height – between 22,000 and 8,000 feet.

Flight Lieutenant D. Fulford, who won the DFC that day, was airborne at 0652, with Flight Sergeant Rawnsley and Sergeant

Walton making up his 'Emerald' Section, and described the battle thus:

'We climbed to 15,000 feet over base. I was told to fly out on a vector of 100 degrees to meet a strong plot of aircraft 30 miles from the coast. I flew behind some cumulus cloud to protect my eyes from the sun and almost immediately sighted the enemy aircraft. They were at 15,000 feet and flying due west, straight at the harbour and I saw two formations of twin-engined bombers, each comprising two vics of seven in line astern, escorted by a number of Navy O's.

'A moment later I sighted another similar formation, about a mile behind. The escorting fighters were not in a definite formation, but spread out all round the bombers, a number being at 20,000 feet and well behind the first formation. I saw the sun glinting on their perspex above and behind me, so 'I promptly brought the section together into a tight vic and climbed north behind some cloud. I climbed to 22,000 feet and then turned west until I was over the rear formation. I saw several enemy fighters weaving behind the formation, so we dived down and selected one machine each.'

Fulford thus took the greatest care to put his section into a favourable situation. It is clear that once they began their attacks on the Japanese planes the section was irretrievably broken up. We will follow the fate of Walton and Rawnsley in due course. Meanwhile Flight Lieutenant Fulford's report continues.

'I dived down behind my enemy aircraft and opened fire from dead astern, firing a five second burst and closing to almost point blank range. Part of the aircraft broke off, I think the hood. The enemy aircraft spun down emitting white smoke or vapour. At about 12,000 feet the machine came out of the spin and began to dive steeply. Several seconds later the starboard wing broke off. The machine went into a vicious spin and fell towards the sea.

'By this time I was climbing quickly and saw six other enemy aircraft climbing after me. I turned so that I was vertically over them, but they climbed very steeply in tight circles and began firing at me. The fire came from both wings[1] and the guns left a trail of

---

[1] This was true of the two cannon. The breech blocks of the two machine guns were in the cockpit.

white smoke. I could see their tracers coming at me and curving away behind. When at 22,000 feet I decided I could not outclimb them, the nearest being about 500 feet below, so I turned over on my back and went vertically down, doing aileron turns. My top speed was 420 m.p.h. (indicated) when I began to pull out at 7,000 feet.

'I finally pulled out at 2,000 feet and flew north in cloud. Having shaken off the enemy aircraft I began to climb away northwards to 15,000 feet, when I turned south again and arrived several miles east of the harbour at 24,000 feet. Having only 10 gallons in each main tank and an empty reserve, I was about to dive away and land when I saw a ragged formation of single-engined bombers at about 7,000 feet, loosely escorted by odd Navy O's, which were weaving above and behind them, flying south-east away from the harbour. I throttled back and dived down on the rearmost fighter, closing from astern and emptying my ammunition into him from about 500 yards to 100 yards. The enemy aircraft immediately turned on its back and dived straight into the sea, 5 miles south-east of Foul Point.

'I followed him down to sea level and flew west round the south side of the harbour and landed at China Bay.'

Rawnsley, brought by Fulford into a superior attacking position says, 'My leader signalled with his wings to attack in echelon and we dived on the weavers at 16,000 feet. I took the extreme starboard enemy aircraft and gave a long burst (3 seconds) directly I had him in my sights. As I broke away he was disintegrating and going down.'

Walton was not heard of again and was killed. Flight Sergeant Rawnsley 'saw No. 2 of my section with white smoke coming from either side of his engine.'

Rawnsley himself was then attacked. 'Cannon shells exploded close to my cockpit, filling it with oil. I came in to land at base with a Navy O behind me. My undercarriage was unserviceable but I managed a safe crash landing.'

As the plane skidded to a final standstill in a cloud of dust, Flight Lieutenant Edsall rushed across to help. The following Zero blazed away and seriously injured Edsall.

For all their early warning, 261 did not fare much better than the

Colombo squadrons. The odds were far too great against them. Eight of the Hurricanes were shot down and another, besides Rawnsley's, was damaged beyond repair when it crashed on landing. Sergeant Pearce, as well as Sergeant Walton, was killed and four others injured, including the CO. One Fulmar, flown by Flying Officer Gregg, from 273 Squadron also failed to return from the day's operations.

Even with due warning our fighters did not manage to disrupt the Japanese attack. Their bombers reached the harbour at 7.20. Their disappointment at finding no fleet was great indeed. What shipping was present, however, was attacked with their usual ruthless efficiency. The *Erebus* was hit many times with heavy casualties amongst her small crew and the *Sagaing,* her decks ablaze, had to be beached. Her four aircraft were lost in the flames. The ship's hulk is still there alongside the naval jetty, though no one in Trinco seems to know her story.

Moving across the harbour, the rest of the bombers struck at China Bay aerodrome. Our own fighters, such as were still flying, were not to be seen. They had gone eastwards to intercept and only the odd straggler, limping home as Rawnsley had done, disputed the air with the Japanese.

A good deal of damage was done on the ground. A full petrol bowser went up in flames, an ammunition dump between the two hangars was blown skywards, taking off most of the roof from both hangars, and 261's orderly room was knocked flat. One stick of bombs fell between the officers' mess and quarters up on the hill and the splinter marks remain in the concrete still. On the ground three men were killed and six wounded.

One Japanese flyer deliberately crashed his plane into one of the Navy's huge fuel tanks just north of the aerodrome. This was two years before the Kamikaze squadrons of suicide pilots were formed, but it is quite clear from contemporary reports that this Japanese was in no way harassed or under pressure. After carefully circling the area he plunged unerringly into the tank, igniting his own funeral pyre which was to blaze in spectacular fashion for days. There were not many tanks which were full, but this happened to be one of them.

While the Japanese bombers, having won complete mastery of

the skies, looked fruitlessly for worthwhile targets, a seaplane from the battleship *Haruna* had come upon the *Hermes,* by now about a hundred miles from Foul Point. Fuchida, illustrating again the strange similarity between events over Trincomalee and over Colombo on the previous Sunday, picked up the sighting report in his 'Kate'.

Again his first reaction was one of alarm. He was not to know that the carrier had not a single airworthy plane on board. He could only think that the fleet was in grave risk of attack, with many of her protecting fighters already engaged at considerable range from their carriers.

'We opened our throttles and sped for home, not without some apprehension.'

In the *Hermes* Captain Onslow realised that they had been spotted and must now expect to be attacked. He turned back towards Trincomalee, moving at the same time obliquely shorewards, and radioed repeatedly for air protection. The Japanese picked up these signals. At China Bay they were in no position to heed his appeals and they do not seem to have been picked up across the island at Ratmalana until much later on.

It was now about 8 a.m. and 150 miles away to the south-west Squadron Leader Ault prepared to lead 11 Squadron's Blenheims into the air to hit back. By 8.20 eleven of them were off and formed up into two flights. Two planes returned with engine trouble, but the remaining nine flew on over the central hills, climbing steadily. Nine Blenheims seem a terribly modest force compared to the huge armadas the Japanese had been able to muster. Two naval observers were carried.

There was no question of a fighter escort, which the Japanese had always had. The Hurricanes from Colombo and Ratmalana had nothing like the range. Those at China Bay were already heavily involved. The attack would have to be made in broad daylight, without fighter protection, and against enormous odds in the air. Leaving the hills behind them they soon crossed the East coast, passing somewhat north of the *Hermes'* position and made for the area from which Thomas had made his dawn sighting.

Fuchida's squadrons had all withdrawn from Trincomalee by 8 o'clock. The casualties we claimed were 5 Bombers and 6 Fighters.

Apart from the Zero which had plunged into the naval fuel tank, none were ever located. They must all have been lost at sea, as were some of our own.

As for the attack on Colombo, Lieutenant Commander Egusa, in the carrier *Hiryu,* was standing by with the remainder of the Japanese aircraft for a possible follow-up attack. At Trincomalee it would clearly not be needed, but once again aerial reconnaissance had found them a better target at the crucial moment.

The Japanese Fleet, finding comparatively little opposition, and being confident that they could evade any naval forces sent against them, if such forces existed (and Admiral Nagumo must by now have harboured some doubts) had come in rather closer than on the Sunday. The distance to the *Hermes* was less than a hundred miles. This time therefore, Nagumo sent off Egusa's second wave before the Trincomalee sortie had been recovered. Over 50 dive-bombers with some 20 fighters made up the force. Weather conditions were again fine and clear.

Over the next hour much was now to happen.

Captain Onslow had continued to steam back towards Trinco, hoping to come within range of fighter protection. His repeated calls for air cover were eventually picked up at Ratmalana, where 8 Fulmars belatedly took off, not much before 10 o'clock.

Soon after this Squadron Leader Ault with his fellow members of 11 Squadron (the crews numbered 27, with the two naval men as supernumeries,) were searching for the Japanese ships. At the same time Egusa's aircraft, about 80 miles to the south-west were approaching the *Hermes*. The last elements of the Trincomalee attack were still landing on. Those already down were being refuelled and rearmed with torpedoes in case the reserve force failed to sink the enemy carrier. Above them a full combat patrol was on the alert.

At 10.25 on the *Akagi,* Admiral Nagumo's flagship, Fuchida tells us that above the hum of activity the alarm suddenly blared out over the loud speakers. Almost immediately, bombs straddled the carrier, slightly ahead, sending up huge columns of water on either side, but not, unhappily, hitting her. Six aircraft identified as 'Wellington bombers' were seen flying over at about 10,000 feet. There may very well have been only the six by then.

When the enemy ships had been sighted, Ault had quickly selected what proved to be the flagship for his attack; but even as they ran up the patrolling Zeros had pounced on them, pouring in a murderous fire. It is a great tribute to the Blenheim crews that their bombs were dropped so accurately under such conditions. With rear gunners doing what they could to hit back, the bombers were now pursued, one flight diving to sea level, the other striving to reach some feeble, but distant cloud cover.

The six 413 Squadron prisoners, strangely enough, were unaware of the attack, although the *Akagi* had been the target. With aero engines running and the general din on the carrier they did not even discern, from their repair well, the nearby bomb detonations. Exultant Japanese later told them that bombers had attacked but added that they had all been shot down. They were not entirely correct.

Shortly after 1 o'clock, four Blenheims, one with an airscrew completely shot away and all damaged, returned to the Racecourse. Squadron Leader Ault's plane was not amongst them; nor did either of the naval observers survive the attack. The other pilots lost were Flying Officer E. Adcock, Pilot Officer R. Knight and Sergeants Stevenson and McClennan. Altogether 17 lives were lost in the operation and, although the Japanese suffered no damage, they recorded that it was the first time Nagumo's Carrier Striking Force had been attacked, either by surface or air forces, since Pearl Harbour four months before.

When the Japanese on the *Akagi* reported to Birchall and his fellow prisoners the abortive attack, they also disclosed that a Catalina had been sighted as the Trincomalee attackers had taken off at dawn and had been shot down into the sea with no survivors. Squadron Leader Birchall could only wonder who it could have been. In fact it was his friend 'Tommy' Thomas, though he would not learn this till the end of the war; 'the most enthusiastic flyer I have ever met, and only happy as long as he was flying or talking about it'. Thomas and his crew could have had little chance, with the skies thick with enemy aircraft.

At almost the same time that the Blenheims' bombs were falling around the *Akagi* the Japanese second wave sighted the *Hermes*. They were amazed to find her entirely unprotected from the air.

The Navy 99 dive-bombers went into line astern and plunged into the attack, following each other down with only a few hundred feet between each.

'We were altering helm every few minutes, twisting and turning to deflect the aim of the pilots,' recalls Lieutenant Dennis Brimble, 2nd Gunnery Officer in the *Hermes,* 'but an aircraft carrier is no destroyer, which is better adapted for this sort of thing. *Hermes* was never built for this type of warfare. At full speed we could only squeeze out some 23 knots and her old design helped not at all. The 4-inch gun on the flight deck aft of the funnel opened up as soon as the first aircraft came into range and, as it dived lower, the Oerlikons too commenced chattering. They seemed to have no effect at all. The Japanese came in so low that, after dropping their bombs, they were in serious danger of being blown to bits by blast of their own making. Those in the lookout position in the fighting top, some 120 feet above the flight deck, remarked later that some planes swept by below their level.

'Suddenly the group called off the attack and disappeared towards the distant shore. *Hermes* continued at full speed towards this same shore line with the object, it is presumed, of reaching shallow water, where the submarines which we thought might be in the vicinity, would have less opportunity of attacking with torpedoes. The ship kept on this course for some half an hour.

'During this short lull, for that is all it amounted to, we took stock of ourselves. The two Oerlikon gunners on the after lift of the flight deck had both been killed. The two 4-inch guns on the flight deck had been put out of action, their crews all being dead or wounded. One of them, with the crew, simply went clean over the side.

'The bombs used by the Japanese were delay-fused, with the result that they penetrated the flight deck and burst in the hangar underneath or entered the engine room.

'Suddenly at a great height appeared flight after flight of planes, estimated to number about 70, and wishful-thinkers thanked God for the RAF. But we were very quickly disillusioned. They used the same tactics as the previous group, coming in one after another in a constant stream, so that as one stick of bombs exploded, the next was already in the air from the following plane. The forward lift rose into the air to a height of approximately 20 feet, snapped its hydraulic stem, dropped half back on to the flight deck and half down the lift well, to wipe out all those in the hangar who had been blown forward by blast.

'We were now on fire from end to end, and sinking. Still they came on.

'Word came at last, "Every man for himself."

'It was a few moments after this order had been given that the bridge received a direct hit and it is believed that it was then that Captain Onslow died. It appears that he went into his cabin under the bridge to collect something or other. No one in that area got out alive.

'The sinking ship, riddled with bombs, on fire from end to end, still drove on towards the shore line, some eight miles away. The flight deck, at a steep angle to port, spewed survivors into the water, so that clusters of men were gathered over a wide area. Almost all boats and life-saving equipment had been smashed by the bombing and I saw only half of one Carley float on the calm water.'

One of those to lose his life from the bomb blast which killed Captain Onslow was Commander Michael Henstock, one of whose brothers, Francis, was a tea planter on the Island. The other, George, also a planter in civilian life, had disappeared in the fighting in Malaya. In fact he had been overrun with an Indian infantry unit, had been bowled over by a Japanese grenade and made to witness the systematic bayonetting of his wounded troops.

At a point only some five miles from the coast the *Hermes* finally plunged, still burning, beneath the waves into thirty fathoms of water.

The *Vampire*, still in company, had seen it all before for she was with the *Prince of Wales* and *Repulse* and had fished out survivors until her deck could take no more. This time she herself was not spared and, after receiving several bomb hits, was sunk even closer inshore. Eight men including her Captain were lost.

Further north the tanker *British Sergeant*, the *Athelstane* and *Hollyhock,* all making for Trincomalee again, were successively sent to the bottom by the bombers.

Just as the elated Japanese airmen were turning away, the 8 Fulmars, having flown across the breadth of Ceylon, arrived on the scene and plunged gamely into the attack. There was a brief engagement in which two of the Fulmars were lost.

AA gunners in the *Hermes,* as well as the Fulmar crews, claimed to have shot down enemy planes, though Japanese accounts do not speak of any losses.

Soon after 11 o'clock, Lieutenant Commander Egusa, much pleased with results, led his formations back to the carriers, leaving many survivors floundering in the sea, with the smoke from the *Hermes* lingering over the scene of her destruction.

The burning oil tank back at China Bay still spewed forth quantities of black smoke into the blue sky and, amidst scenes of destruction, comparative peace and quiet at last reigned at Trincomalee.

The morning's events had been almost a carbon copy of the Easter Sunday attack.

While the day's engagements were being fought out on the East Coast, Admiral Somerville, with Force A, was moving northwards from Addu Atoll to Bombay. In the event the Eastern Fleet had made not a single offensive move against the Japanese. It was scarcely a situation Somerville could relish. Had it been otherwise historians of the future would not be able to aver, as they doubtless will, that the last major action ever to be fought by the Royal Navy with a fleet of comparable size was at Trafalgar. For such a fleet will never sail again under the White Ensign and the only opportunity for such a battle to present itself in World War II was here in the Indian Ocean. The engagement between the German High Seas Fleet and the British Grand Fleet at Jutland in 1916, in spite of disproportionate losses, never developed beyond an indecisive skirmish before darkness overtook the ships and contact between the two forces was lost.

It is perhaps as well. The fearful increase in naval fire power since Nelson's day would have meant carnage on a terrible scale if a major fleet action had been fought on either occasion. The great weight of lethal explosives carried around in the magazines of modern ships of the line made them vulnerable targets, liable to be blown to pieces, as the *Hood* was, by a single salvo with (virtually) every man jack aboard; and in a battleship that amounts to twelve to fourteen hundred men.

It was Churchill who said that at Jutland Admiral Jellicoe had the chance to lose the war in the course of a single afternoon. Might not Admiral Somerville have had in mind that, with the Eastern Fleet in his care, he had been placed in the same unenviable position?

For the *Hermes* survivors and the other victims of the morning's sinkings, rescue would clearly not come from the ships of Force A. Somerville had signalled to the Admiralty 'Am not prepared to send another warship to this area without fighter protection at present.' Yet in the end they fared better than the men from the *Dorsetshire* and *Cornwall*. For quite soon after the sinkings the small hospital ship *Vita*, coming up from the south, appeared on the scene and spent the rest of the morning and much of the early afternoon combing the sea for survivors from the various sinkings. When at length she could find no more she turned south and made for Colombo. One group of seven sailors had a much more difficult time. All from the *Hermes*, they decided soon after their ship had gone down that their best hope was to swim for the shore, five miles away, and keeping in company began the long haul.

When, at some distance, a ship could be seen moving among the men left behind in the water they concluded it was Japanese. They were not prepared to be captured and, keeping together and refusing to leave any flagging member of the company behind, they swam on, making very slow progress.

At last when it was almost dusk and they were completely exhausted, they came to a navigational buoy some little way outside the harbour at Batticaloa. Too weak to do anything more, they secured themselves to the buoy and stuck it out for the whole night, when a small boat, manned by local fishermen, came upon them and took them ashore.

Nagumo had already sent back his oilers and supply ships. Ozawa could find no more targets in the Bay of Bengal and both task forces turned to retire between the Andaman and Nicobar Islands.

Ceylon's trials were over.

This is not to say that the fact was appreciated on the island. There was however a general sense of elation, though not for the correct reasons. Our fighter aircraft had taken a severe knock and the morale of the survivors must have suffered from the mauling they had received. It had been brought suddenly home to them that the Japanese were tough customers, their planes of better performance than they had been led to expect and their flyers much more efficient. Yet they believed they had inflicted heavy casualties and the Japs had been given a sound hiding, or, in Churchill's expressive phrase 'they had come in contact with bone'.

No naval forces were left in Ceylon. That much was clear to all. Although it was soon learnt that the *Hermes* had been sunk off the east coast, the fate of the *Dorsetshire* and *Cornwall* was known to very few. No one could say where the fleet were, but there was confidence that they were at hand. Even to the Armed Services in Ceylon it would have come as an unpleasant surprise to learn that the Eastern Fleet had already been ordered to retire from the theatre and not under any circumstances to return to Ceylon harbours.

Invasion had seemed a distinct possibility a week ago. This after all had been the inevitable result of every Japanese venture so far. But now, in ignorance of the facts, there was a general feeling that they had been soundly repulsed and there was some understandable optimism. In war, almost more than in other spheres, the truth has less significance in men's minds than what they feel to be true.

In London on the 10th the Chiefs of Staff met, 'mainly concerned in trying to save India from the Japs'.[1] For they too had yet to appreciate that the main threat was over.

Churchill, writing as the 'Former Naval Person' to President Roosevelt put a braver face on things than he was doing in the Cabinet:

> I believe that any junction between the Japanese and Germans is going to take a great deal of doing but realise that the remote prospect of this is something to be watched. In the meantime, as you will have seen in the Press, we have had a good crack at Japan by air and I am hoping that we can make it very difficult for them to keep too many of their big ships in the Indian Ocean.

[1] *The Turn of the Tide* – Arthur Bryant (1957)

However he made it clear to the President that 'until we are able to fight a fleet action there is no reason why the Japanese should not become the dominating factor in the Western Indian Ocean.' He suggested that, by sending further American ships across the Atlantic, the Americans could make it possible for British warships to be sent off to re-inforce the Eastern Fleet and retrieve the situation.

Roosevelt was sympathetic, but he had his own offensive operations planned in the Pacific and retrieving British chestnuts out of the fire in the Indian Ocean cannot have fitted in with these. Indeed the diversion from the Pacific of nearly a third of the Japanese battle fleet and half their aircraft carriers could only have relieved the pressure on his own doorstep.

It must have seemed likely that Japanese attentions were still directed westwards for on the 17th April Roosevelt was writing to Churchill: 'A Japanese land attack on Ceylon in my opinion won't be made for several weeks time.'

After remaining at sea for two days, Admiral Somerville and the reduced faster element of his Fleet put into Bombay where a conference of the naval military, air force and civil powers was held. General Wavell, the C-in-C, was terribly disillusioned with the situation at sea. He had been encouraged to expect great things of the fleet and was now brought down to earth by the admitted fact that we had lost all semblance of control of the Indian Ocean except off the African coast. Although Admiral Somerville had been told to hold the Fleet in readiness to deal with any inferior force which might venture into the Indian Ocean, to the Japanese there was not now the slightest need to send out such a force.

At Bombay the Indian element of Convoy WS 16 now arrived after an uneventful voyage lasting two months. But reinforcements in this convoy were not of a type to relieve the present situation.

Understandably Wavell called for more planes and protested that naval forces were not, it now seemed, sufficient to protect India or Ceylon from invasion. To him it seemed highly probable that the Japanese, having probed our defences, would now return with occupation troops. He contrasted No 11 Squadron's pathetic efforts with the huge raids then being mustered against Germany by Bomber Command and questioned if the Chiefs of Staff Committee were serious in their desire to hang on to India.

He got little sympathy. For we were now committed to a new step, planned some weeks before, Operation Ironclad, for which all available reinforcements were being diverted and for which Wavell's resources in India were even to be to some extent depleted. The Chiefs of Staff, rightly as Wavell himself, to his credit, was later to admit, soon deemed the threat to India and Ceylon, both by sea and by land, to have receded.

One last blow was to be delivered against the Japanese before the Indian Ocean was to resume its normal tranquillity. A Hudson aircraft from Akyab, on the northern coast of Burma, close to the Indian border, carrying out a reconnaissance of Port Blair in the Andamans on the 11th April, found nine flying boats at their moorings. Two Hudsons attacked these on the 14th, sank one and left two burning. On the 18th they tried again and claimed two destroyed and three damaged. This time, however, Zero fighters took off and shot down one of the Hudsons.

On the same day the Ceylon contingent of Convoy WS 16, accommodated for the last leg of the voyage, from Bombay, in a single troopship, the *Devonshire,* arrived at Colombo. With recent events fresh in everyone's minds, anti-submarine watches had been most dutifully kept by all on board. Not a flying fish disturbed the glassy blue surface of the sea (and there were plenty of them) but several pairs of sharp eyes followed its shallow trajectory and marked the terminal splash as it returned to the water. On one of these watches I recall a moment of some irony. Stationed astern, beside what was probably the ship's sole armament, an old 4-inch gun, I found it inscribed 'Nagasaki – 1919' – a relic of that earlier war when Japan had been aligned with us.

The ocean was understandably empty after the last three weeks' excitement. One of the few north-bound merchantmen to be passed was the *Anglo-Canadian* (Captain Williams). She had on board the party of escapees from Singapore who had sailed from Padang in the *Sederhana Djohanis*. The *Anglo-Canadian* had come across her within sight of the Ceylon coast. She had passed quite unscathed through the area of the Japanese First Carrier Fleet's manoeuvrings.

At Colombo, as the *Devonshire* approached, a pall of smoke hung over the harbour where the *Hector* continued to burn. By now it seemed that the Japanese were far away. But no one really knew. However the docks were still devoid of labour and a large element of Colombo's population was gone. They would only begin to trickle back some weeks later. The newly arrived troops had to row themselves ashore in the ship's boats.

In much the same way as they had at Singapore, we found ourselves deposited at Colombo in a strange tropical land. Few of us had ever left Europe before. The climate was hot and humid and we had been over two months confined in troopships, only being released ashore twice. A new life, in almost every accepted sense of the word, was about to begin for us all. This time there seemed perhaps less of an emergency than there had been at Singapore but a return of the Japanese in the near future seemed highly probable. We would now prepare to retaliate as soon as it was needed. I doubt if any of us guessed that, save for the few who moved on to Burma, this would take another full three years.

The author, who certainly harboured no suspicion that he would remain in the island for over 27 years, took up duties at the combined Naval and Air Operations Room at Colombo where one of the Air Controllers, newly promoted to Squadron Leader, was Bill Bradshaw who had so capably shadowed the Japanese Fleet on Easter Sunday morning, only two weeks before.

General Wavell, accompanying Admiral Somerville in the *Warspite*, disembarked at Colombo for discussions with Admiral Layton and the other service chiefs. The Eastern Fleet then made for the Seychelles, from which they sailed on to Kilindini, near Mombasa.

Admiral Nagumo and his First Carrier Striking Force, having refuelled at Singapore, was approaching home waters on the 18th.

A fortnight after the alarm had been raised in Ceylon there was now, from a naval point of view, a total vacuum in the Bay of Bengal and the Indian Ocean.

CHAPTER NINE

The Outlook Broadens

'Midway . . . the battle that doomed Japan'.
COMMANDER MITSUI FUCHIDA

At this juncture the focus of the war with Japan switches to the Pacific, where the Americans, 'the sleeping giant,' awoken at Pearl Harbour, would soon come into their own and Japan would be made to pay dearly for her early triumphs.

Our particular narrative is not quite done, however.

As Nagumo left Formosa behind and approached Kyushu and home, another, rather smaller, fleet, a thousand miles eastwards was pressing at best speed westwards towards Japan. The US Task Force 16, under Vice-Admiral William F. Halsey, Junior, was about to strike the first retaliatory blow. Consisting of the aircraft carriers *Enterprise* and *Hornet* with four cruisers (*Northampton, Salt Lake City, Vincennes* and *Nashville*) and attendant destroyers and oilers, Task Force 16's objective was Tokyo itself.

The Americans had been determined to take offensive action ever since Pearl Harbour and had used every ingenuity to take the one conceivable retaliation possible.

Carrier-borne planes then, as now, have a limited range and the Americans had no aircraft capable of reaching Japan and returning to carriers except by taking enormous risks and running the carriers in so close that they would be subjecting them to the same fate as the *Prince of Wales* and *Repulse*. A daring plan was therefore conceived of sending off twin-engined *Army* B-25 Mitchell Bombers to do the trip one way and to fly on to Chinese bases. With the element of surprise to assist them it was planned to approach to within 500 miles of the coast of Japan.

With maximum fuel loads being carried by each plane and quite a proportion of the flight deck of the *Hornet* taken up by the 16 Mitchells, too large to be parked below, it was going to be a tremendous feat to get them airborne.

There were numerous difficulties.

For reasons of security and because of difficulties in communication, arrangements with Chiang Kai Shek and the Chinese were never properly completed. Seas were unusually heavy and Admiral Halsey was dismayed to be sighted where no shipping would normally be expected by Japanese patrol boats on three successive occasions in the early hours of the 18th April. For surprise seemed absolutely essential.

Admiral Yamamoto, the Japanese Naval C-in-C, had expected retaliatory action by the Americans ever since Pearl Harbour. That it would be in the form of a carrier-borne air attack seemed almost certain. He therefore posted small picket boats along a line extending over a thousand miles from north to south, 700 miles East of Japan, with the sole task of flashing a radio warning of the approach of any such force. An ex-fishing trawler, the *Nitto Maru*, was the first to sight the Americans and duly got off a signal. She was sunk soon after.

Ultimately, because complete surprise had not proved possible, the bombers were despatched some 125 miles farther out than planned, which was to stretch their endurance almost beyond their limits and would bring them over Tokyo, Nagoya, Osaka and Kobe in daylight instead of at night as planned. It was asking a great deal of the airmen, for all of whom it would be their first war flight, but they gallantly agreed.

Led by Lieutenant Colonel Jimmy Doolittle, all 16 Mitchells managed to stagger off the carrier, to which there was no hope of returning. It was a feat of amazing boldness. The task force immediately turned away for home at full speed and the bombers were left to their own devices, with 1,000 miles to go and landings at unfamiliar Chinese airfields ahead of them in dusk or darkness. Under the original plan this would have been in broad daylight.

Assigned targets were strictly of a military nature. But there was not enough fuel for searching them out and some bombs doubtless fell inaccurately. The Americans flew in at minimum height.

By an unkind stroke of fate, Tokyo was having a practice air-raid alert that day, with mock attacks by Japanese planes. Thus many people thought it all part of the show and the psychological effects of the attack were partly nullified in consequence. The bombers were spread very thinly to cover as many targets as possible and, apart from Tokyo, bombs fell on Yokohama, Kawasaki, Yokosuka, Nagoya, Yokkaichi, Wakayama and Kobe.

The Japanese had made some quick calculations as soon as the *Nitto Maru's* signal had been received and on the known range of carrier-borne aircraft, it was anticipated that the Americans would not be within striking range before the following day, the 19th. It is unlikely that full defensive precautions had been taken on the 18th. There were quite heavy fighter defences in the Tokyo area which had been recently reinforced; but they were taken by surprise. Opposition from them and from AA gunfire was feeble.

There were no American casualties at all over Japan, but the aircrews' trials had scarcely begun. They had now to eke out their last remaining fuel and to try and locate completely strange Chinese bases.

One plane, making for Vladivostok, put down at Primorsky in Southern Siberia. Although Russia and the United States had been Allies now for over four months, internment is what faced the crew. This strange step was taken in conformity with the Non-Aggression Treaty which still subsisted between Japan and Russia and which it was much in Russia's interest to foster. Other planes were fired on by the Chinese. At Chuchow airfield all lights were extinguished in the belief that the approaching aircraft were hostile and the Mitchells' crews were consequently compelled to make crash landings or to bail out over inhospitable mountain country. Five Americans were killed in this way.

According to Charles E. Bohlen, who was at that time Second Secretary at the US Embassy in Tokyo, where he was confined at the time of the raid, one stick of bombs struck a hospital, causing casualties. This may perhaps be the reason why a number of airmen, captured by the Japanese, were sentenced to death by a military court. Three were executed after allegations that they had indulged in the terror bombing of civilians. Yet out of the 75 who took part in this audacious raid 66 survived the war (one dying as a prisoner of war). The Russians finally placed no solid obstacles in the way of the five interned airmen escaping to Iran.

Because the Mitchells were army planes and not of a type to be operated from aircraft-carriers, the Japanese High Command were at first completely perplexed by the attack and could not make out whence it had been launched. Only when reports came in from China late in the day were they able to piece together the details of the operation. Japanese bombers had been launched in retaliation and flew a search eastwards to the limit of their endurance without sighting the enemy task force, which returned to Pearl Harbour unmolested.

Although the material results were modest and the Americans lost all the attacking Mitchells, the raid alarmed the Japanese Imperial High Command.

The dreadful vengeance wreaked on the Chinese in the Chekiang Province where most of the American flyers came down and were succoured by the local inhabitants has received comparatively little publicity. Whole villages were razed and the number of killed is said to have run into thousands.

The impact of the Tokyo raid on the minds of the Japanese naval leaders hardened their determination to thrust eastwards and did much to overcome the scruples of any who had advocated holding back. Operations against Midway Island, being planned at that moment, were immediately ordered.

A few days after the Doolittle raids (as they came to be known), Admiral Nagumo's fleet, which had been alerted for possible retaliation against Admiral Halsey's ships, reached Yokohama, bringing with them Squadron Leader Birchall and the remainder of his Catalina crew. It was miserable luck for them to arrive at such a time. It was the 22nd April and the population of Japan had had time to work up to the full their indignation at the air raids, the horrors of which had been much magnified by the press and official accounts; there was great apprehension too at the wholly unexpected appearance of enemy bombers over Japan itself.

After being paraded through the streets, reviled and knocked about by the civilian population, they were led away to endure for over three years the harsh conditions of imprisonment by the Japanese.

Whilst Nagumo moved back to Japan to prepare for new operations in the Pacific, British forces now began to concentrate their attention on the Indian Ocean's westward shores.

Operation Ironclad, now to be embarked upon, was the code

name for the occupation of Diego Suarez, the excellent base at the northern extremity of Madagascar, together with the occupation of as much territory as would be needed to secure the unhindered use of the harbour.

With the Mediterranean closed to us and all material reinforcements, both for the Middle East and India, being routed round the Cape, Madagascar sitting firmly between the Mozambique Channel and the more open eastward route, commanded the shipping lanes along which every man and every item of equipment must pass. The very thought of hostile influences at work in such a place was unbearable.

Allied Intelligence, thanks to the Americans' cracking of the Japanese diplomatic code, was very well informed at this time and, within a remarkably short time of the voicing of Japanese intentions to their German Allies, both as to Ceylon and Madagascar, we were taking such counter measures as we could. In fact it is now clear that Japan was more intent on placating and heartening Germany than on actually extending her influence so far westwards, for Nagumo's sortie to Ceylon waters and Japanese interference in the Madagascar campaign, with which we will shortly be dealing, fell much short of what had been expected by the Germans. The Vichy Government had, however, as early as November 1941, submitted to German pressure and agreed to Japanese occupation of the island if it became necessary.

Writing over thirty years after the event, with all the advantages of hindsight, it is hard to take seriously the threat to Madagascar which was thought to be developing now that Japan had entered the Indian Ocean.

This huge island, nearly a thousand miles long, which lies off the East coast of Africa, had remained loyal to Vichy, although de Gaulle was persuaded that strong elements leaned towards his Free French movement.

The tragedies enacted at Oran and Dakar were fresh in everyone's memories. Added to this the strange attitude towards de Gaulle of Roosevelt and, to a less extent, of Churchill. It is difficult to believe now that the acknowledged twentieth century saviour of France was accorded no recognition at all by the United States until D-Day, and then only with undisguised reluctance, and that he was excluded from much of the Allies' planning even after the Normandy landings. Both Roosevelt and Churchill, for a variety of reasons, sought for much of the War to find a French leader to supplant de Gaulle and his rancour survived to colour his attitude to the United States and Britain right up to his death.

Vichy France had allowed Japan the use of bases in Indo-China and there was a danger that she would do the same in Madagascar. The all-important sea route round the Cape could thus be made untenable. It was important therefore that the Allies should forestall such a move. De Gaulle himself had suggested it and was keen to send a Free French occupation force.

Now that three quarters of the Indian Ocean had been yielded to the Japanese, the African coast, at least, had to be made secure. There were, after the retirement adequate naval forces available, though comparatively few of the Eastern Fleet's units were to be involved. For a separate fleet, detached from Force H, had been mustered for Ironclad, under Admiral Syfret. The *Indomitable* took the place of the sunken *Hermes* and the battleship *Ramillies* was detached to lend her support, with the destroyers *Paladin* and *Panther* in company.

Otherwise the occupation force (Force 121) was to move in from the Atlantic, concentrating first at Durban. However the *Formidable* and other units of Admiral Somerville's Fleet maintained protective patrols well east of the island during the opening stages of the operation to guard against any Japanese interference.

The initial landings were made early on the morning of 5th May.

De Gaulle, to his chagrin, had not been consulted, nor even informed. There was hope that resistance would be half-hearted if the British carried out the operation alone. It was only one of the many slights which de Gaulle would never forget. By the time the whole of Madagascar was secured, which in the end proved necessary and was not to be completed until the following November, largely by South African forces, de Gaulle had perforce to be brought in.

Diego Suarez itself was quickly secured, but to Churchill's disappointment French resistance was fairly stiff.

The moment had now come for the Japanese to implement their promise, made through Admiral Nomura in Berlin, to operate off the East coast of Africa. The firm decision had been taken that the Indian Ocean was of only minor importance to the Japanese and their major fleet units would have to remain in the Pacific, but there were many excellent prizes to be had for their submarines, and the 1st Division of their 8th Submarine Flotilla, normally based at Kwajalein in the Marshall Islands, left Penang towards the end of April under Rear Admiral Ishizaki.

The Japanese had built a series of much larger submarines than any of the other powers, each in the neighbourhood of 2,000 tons (the largest German U-Boat at this time was some 1,600 tons). These were not very manoeuvrable but had a high surface speed and long range. Furthermore they were designed to carry a midget submarine or small reconnaissance float-plane. This enormously increased their scope and range. Such submarines had been used at Pearl Harbour, and their satellite midgets had gained access into the harbour some time before the raid started. Indeed, one was sighted and depth-charged by an American destroyer an hour beforehand, though no one could bring themselves to believe it was a hostile submarine.

Five of these 2,000 ton boats, *I–10, I–16, I–18, I–20* and *I–30*, made up Admiral Ishizaki's division and two supply ships, *Aikoku Maru* and *Hokaku Maru,* moved out into the southern Indian Ocean to rendezvous with them later. One of these later captured the 8,000 ton Dutch tanker *Genota* some 500 miles SSE of Diego Garcia (in the Chagos Archipelago, not to be confused with Diego Suarez).

I–30 went northwards, arriving off Aden on the 7th May where her float-plane reconnoitred the harbour. She moved slowly south, carrying out similar reconnaissances at Djibuti, Zanzibar and Dar-es-Salaam, but nothing was sighted to merit attention.

Of the remainder, *I–10* had a float-plane and the other three carried midget submarines. Greatly daring, the plane flew up the Natal coast and appeared off Durban in the early hours of 20th May. She was challenged, replied with the wrong letter of the day and disappeared seawards. It is hardly surprising that no one could imagine where the plane had come from. Perhaps it was suspected to be a French machine from Madagascar. Most likely people scratched their heads and wondered if it had all been imagined. There are countless such unexplained incidents in wartime.

Admiral Ishizaki and his four submarines were all off Diego Suarez by the evening of the 29th May, by which time the harbour was full of British shipping. *I–10,* in which Ishizaki carried his flag, despatched her float-plane and it arrived in the dusk over the harbour. The alarm was raised, for it was suspected to be a Vichy French plane. The *Ramillies* hauled up her anchor, vacated her berth and moved slowly and evasively about the huge harbour. Of the three available midget submarines one could not be launched because of engine trouble, but both *I–16* and *I–18* got theirs away.

As at Pearl Harbour it was recognised by the Japanese, midget submarine crews included, that the chances of a return to the mother ships were negligible. Long before the Kamikaze squadrons of suicide pilots were formed there seem to have been sufficient Japanese with the necessary courage and patriotism to make this sacrifice. Since to fall into the hands of the enemy was considered the supreme disgrace their chances of survival were that much slimmer. One crew member did in fact fall into American hands after the Pearl Harbour attack, but otherwise in the three most noteworthy operations by miniature submarines, namely Pearl Harbour, Diego Suarez and a similar operation in Sydney Harbour which was a miserable failure; no one survived.

At least one midget submarine must have gained access to Diego Suarez harbour for a torpedo struck the *Ramillies* at 8.25 p.m. and another the 7,000 ton *British Loyalty* an hour later.

One of the midgets ran aground and a second failed to return, its fate still being unknown. Two men, the crew of one of these, located a few nights later by a commando patrol, refused to surrender and were shot. The grounded submarine was not discovered till mid-June.

Fortunately the *Ramillies* managed to return to Durban under her own steam. Here was another opportunity for the Admiralty to learn the bitter lesson, that the day of the big capital ship was over; that the main consideration henceforth would be to keep such ships out of harm's way. No doubt sailors would continue to chant between the mess decks:

Roll out the *Nelson,* the *Rodney,* the *Hood,*
For the whole ruddy Air Force is no effing good.

But they could not have been more wrong. [1]

The *British Loyalty,* having settled on the bottom, was later repaired, only to be struck in 1944 by another Japanese torpedo whilst at anchor at Addu Atoll, where a submarine had ingeniously fired through a gap in the atoll.

Succoured and refuelled by their two supply ships, which remained well clear of Madagascar to the east and south-east, the Japanese submarines then operated in the Mozambique Channel and elsewhere along the East African coast, where they spent most of the next two months. They enjoyed considerable success, returning safely to Penang in early August with the sinking of 120,000 tons of merchant shipping to their credit, as well as the damage inflicted on the *Ramillies.* This put her out of action for several months.

The *Hokaku Maru* and *Aikoku Maru,* in addition to the capture of one ship, already mentioned, themselves sank two others.

They had, of course, lost in return two midget submarines and their crews (two men each). The cost to the Japanese was not therefore very heavy.

But whilst Diego Suarez was being secured, the first major battle in the Pacific between the Japanese and the Americans was being fought. Known as the Battle of the Coral Sea, it was in some ways an inconclusive battle, losses being fairly evenly divided. However Japanese naval intentions were to support landings of troops at Port Moresby in New Guinea and the troopships were forced to turn back. Their advance to the south-east was thus halted and the threat to Australia relieved.

The battle set the pattern for the remainder of the war, since no ship from either fleet came within visual range of the other. Only the crews of small carrier-borne aircraft were to sight the enemy and to them went the credit for all the losses inflicted.

The Americans lost the carrier *Lexington* and the *Yorktown* was damaged. The Japanese lost the light carrier *Shoho* and the *Shokaku*

---

[1] Actually a modified version was being sung by 1942:
'Roll out the *Nelson,* the *Rodney, Renown*
You can't have the *Hood* as the b——'s gone down.'
Even airmen were prepared to sing this version.

was badly damaged. Three quarters of the planes from the *Shokaku* and *Zuikaku* were lost.

Thus, in the Battle of the Coral Sea, began the steady destruction by the United States Navy of virtually the whole of the Japanese fleet which had swept the Indian Ocean so confidently and with such devastating success in April 1942.

But to the Japanese at this stage this was, after all, their first and only setback. The carriers *Hiryu* (the name means Flying Dragon) and *Soryu* (Green Dragon) and the *Akagi* (Red Castle) were busy refitting in Japan after the Indian Ocean sortie and took no part in the Coral Sea Battle. Together with the *Kaga* (Increased Joy) they were being got ready for what was to prove the crucial battle of the Pacific War in which neither the *Shokaku* (Soaring Crane) nor the *Zuikaku* (Happy Crane) could take part after their mauling by the Americans.

Repairs to the *Yorktown*, on the other hand, were so swiftly carried out at Pearl Harbour that she was able to play an important role in the next battle – The Battle of Midway. If she had been absent things would almost certainly have gone the other way. For by now it was accepted that aircraft carriers counted, and carriers only. The efficiency of the shipwrights and repair gangs at Pearl Harbour may therefore be the root cause for the turning of the tables on the Japanese. For it was only in the last few hours of this crucial contest that, in quick succession, the *Akagi, Kaga, Soryu* and *Hiryu* were all sunk, and with them went veteran airmen and skilled maintenance crews who would never be replaced.

The Americans themselves lost the *Yorktown*, but in the course of a single day, exactly two months after the Easter Sunday raid, Nagumo's Carrier Striking Force had been reduced to an insignificant remnant. Many of the flyers who had pounded Colombo, Trincomalee, the *Dorsetshire, Cornwall* and *Hermes* were lost in this engagement.

The effects of the Battle of Midway were such as to preclude once and for all a Japanese victory in the War and this was immediately understood by the Imperial High Command even though not admitted. It is significant that in the summer of 1941, before the decision was made to attack America, Admiral Yamamoto was realist enough to tell Prime Minister Konoye frankly:

'If you tell me that it is necessary that we fight, then in the first six months to a year of War against the United States and England I will run wild, and I will show you an uninterrupted succession of victories; I must also tell you that, should the war be prolonged for two or three years, I have no confidence in our ultimate victory.'

Japan's strategy had always been to strike a few massive and decisive blows by which the American naval forces would be destroyed, to seize what territory they required in Asia and the Pacific and to impose a negotiated settlement on a demoralised United States and a Britain wholly occupied by the Germans and Italians in Europe and the Middle East. Japanese planners had decided long since that, with their scanty internal resources, they could not undertake a protracted naval war and must concentrate on the early annihilation of the enemy's fleet.

They came very close to doing this; but when Midway went against them their chance had gone. There was no longer any hope for them, even in spite of the long chain of victories to their credit. Observers who knew Admiral Nagumo well spoke of him retiring morosely into his shell after this defeat.

The Battle of Midway could never have been fought if Egusa's dive bombers had found the *Hornet, Enterprise, Yorktown, Saratoga* and *Lexington,* or even two or three of these carriers, at Pearl Harbour on 7th December. Midway Island would have been occupied by the Japanese, as planned, and a negotiated peace might well have resulted.

Such was the importance of Midway, one of the really decisive battles of history, and significantly fought without a single battleship on the victor's side. It does not form a part of our particular narrative, but it is a splendid story. Walter Lord has covered it very well on the American side and Mitsuo Fuchida for the Japanese. The sub-title Fuchida gave his book is 'The Battle that Doomed Japan'. Which is all very true. A single comment of his is worth quoting:

The advance intelligence which the USA had of the Japanese plan of attack was the foremost single and immediate cause of Japan's defeat.

In another sphere this foreknowledge was to help the Americans.

At the same time that the Battle of Midway was being fought, a diversionary air raid was carried out by a small force of Japanese aircraft from the light carrier *Ryujo* (which had taken part in the northern sortie into the Indian Ocean in April). The target was Dutch Harbour in the Aleutians, where a radio station and pier installations were bombed and flying boats were strafed in the water.

The attack had, in the event, practically no strategic or tactical significance. It was supposed to have diverted American attention northwards from Midway where the real blow was being struck. But the Americans, with the Japanese cypher code cracked, had the most accurate foreknowledge of the plan and were not in any way deceived. Even when Japanese landed on Kiska Island and remained in occupation there for several months in 1943 the Americans did not allow themselves to feel perturbed.

Having carried out their attack on Dutch Harbour, the 11 Type 97 (Kate) Bombers and 6 Zero Fighters reformed for their return to the *Ryujo*, but one Zero pilot, Petty Officer Tadayoshi Koga, found that one of the fuel tanks of his plane was leaking a thin spray of petrol. He had already lost the fuel he would need for his return. Contacting his flight commander, he decided to force land on a small island Akutan, which seemed to be flat and clear, in the hope of being picked up by a Japanese submarine, of which there were several in the area. Alas, the surface of the island was tundra. His friends were dismayed to see the plane tip up onto its nose immediately on touch-down, with no sign of life from the unfortunate Koga and, although a submarine was sent to look for him, no sign of him was found.

An American reconnaissance plane soon sighted the Zero, sticking up conspicuously on the uninhabited island. A ground party was guided to the spot and found the plane only slightly damaged and the pilot dead from a severe blow on the head.

This was an invaluable windfall. Repairs were effected and the Zero was soon flying again under American colours. On being submitted to exhaustive test flights its many excellent qualities were at once appreciated, but, more valuable still, they were able to detect its weaknesses as well. It had no self-sealing tanks, no armour plate and a poor diving performance.

The US Navy at once set to work to eclipse the Zero, which they succeeded in doing when the Grumman Hellcat went into production.

Japan had been wise enough to consider and finally to adopt as early as July 1938 as a standard fitting in naval fighter aircraft the Oerlikon 20 mm. cannon which they manufactured under licence. America, Britain and other powers had all tried this but had not adopted it at this stage. It was now realised how much more damaging the explosive shell could be than the .303 inch solid bullet, even although a fighter aircraft could fire many more of these and at a higher muzzle velocity.

With the Hellcat the Americans would now catch up the Japanese in this field and many later versions of the Hurricane and Spitfire would be similarly armed.

CHAPTER TEN

Sequels and Recriminations

'We never had anything in the last War comparable with
this series of disasters.'

LORD WINTERTON

Recriminations were bound to follow the Indian Ocean operations.
We had survived a severe trial. But there was no glory in it.
Churchill's high hopes of the Eastern Fleet had been swiftly
dashed. Instead of forcing discretion on the Japanese and calling a
halt to their westward expansion, the Fleet had been bustled
ignominiously off the scene, smarting from unexpected losses. He
wasted no time in pouring criticism on the Admiralty and looking
round for possible scapegoats.

Why, he asked, did Japanese carriers accommodate so many
more aircraft than we did? Why were our air-crews always said to
be untrained? Was Admiral Somerville justified in sending the
Dorsetshire and *Cornwall* to Colombo and the *Hermes* and *Vampire* to
Trincomalee? Was it correct to order the *Hermes* and the other
vessels to sail once an air attack was expected? How was this all to
be explained to Parliament and the country?

The First Lord did his best to deal with all these points – not
always very satisfactorily.

He wrote to the Prime Minister on the 12th April:

Nothing in these dispositions or the consequences which
followed from them has in any way weakened the confidence of
the Admiralty in Admiral Somerville's judgement.

I do not consider Somerville is open to criticism for what he
did *at the time*. It would be unfair to assess his action on what we
know now.

Moving the *Hermes* from Trincomalee was the right decision in
the circumstances (Pearl Harbour was still in everyone's minds)

'and it was bad luck that an enemy aircraft which was reconnoitring Colombo [sic] should have detected *Hermes* when she was well clear of Trincomalee.'

Japanese air-crews, it was thought, would put up with cramped quarters which our own crews would not endure. Perhaps additional aircraft were carried as deck cargo, for which there was no accommodation below.

For Britain's Senior Service, with its proud traditions, it had been a shattering loss of face to have retired, sadly mauled, from such an important sphere of operations without ever having engaged the enemy and without so much as a single offensive move. What was worse was to have endured this at the hands of the navy of an Asiatic race, always considered till then (though not since) mere emulators of western ways and not properly in the front rank of the world's martial Powers.

Admiral Somerville found himself loyally and staunchly supported by Sir Dudley Pound, the First Lord of the Admiralty, but now had to bear the brunt of the criticism, though it is clear he had done his best to obey his orders and to fall in with the Chiefs of Staff Committee's rapidly changing attitudes. They, no less than he, had in the short space of ten days, moved from aggressive intent to full flight and a complete abandonment of all initiative in the Indian Ocean. Indeed the major charge against Somerville was that he had needlessly lost the *Hermes* and the two cruisers in the face of orders not to 'stick his neck out'. They sought to place the blame for their loss on his shoulders as a result of the one major decision he seems to have taken on his own. This was to conclude, when no Japanese ships had appeared by 2nd April, that the alarm had been false. His orders to the three ships to return to Ceylon, on the strength of this hasty conclusion, were, in spite of the numerous practical reasons for their going, to cost the Eastern Fleet dear.

To his credit, however, he would not hear of any criticism of the RAF, or countenance the suggestion that there was insufficient liaison between the two Services. He was the first to maintain that, with what little they had, the airmen had acquitted themselves well.

Liaison between the two services was certainly not as close as it should have been, but it must be appreciated that Ceylon had not been considered as a possible war theatre until a comparatively few days before the Japanese fleet appeared over the horizon. Its defensive elements had been hastily thrown together from every quarter and had hardly settled down or found their feet before the blow was upon them.

There was therefore nothing like the organisation on the airfields which flyers had been used to at the Home stations from which many of them had recently come. Flight Lieutenant Hildyard recalls how incensed Flying Officer Graham had been at the lack of organisation at Koggala just before he took off on his last flight.

An important factor was the extreme secrecy which had to be (and fortunately was) maintained over the existence of the base at Addu Atoll. Then again, once the Eastern Fleet was at sea the rigid maintenance of radio silence by every unit of the Fleet made impossible any sort of close liaison with Ceylon. No one can question the wisdom of this, but there were unfortunate consequences.

Aircrews flying from Ceylon could be told only that our own Fleet was in the vicinity. No one was told anything more specific than this and, because the *Formidable* and *Indomitable,* with a full complement of aircraft, were with the Eastern Fleet, there seemed every likelihood that their planes would be encountered. Certainly Ceylon-based flyers expected this with the sad result that enemy aircraft were not recognised as such by the Fleet Air Arm Fulmars or by Bradshaw in his Catalina in the early hours of Easter Sunday.

While Somerville was managing to survive these censures, expressions of general dissatisfaction began to make themselves felt on a much higher level; to the very fountain head of power, in fact.

The Prime Minister had easily swept aside in January a vote of no confidence when but a single vote had been cast against him and no one took this to be anything but a carefully staged demonstration of national support.

During the course of May and early June, however, there occurred in the House of Commons events which do much to explain why Sir Winston Churchill, on looking back over the war, should have deemed the Japanese Indian Ocean sortie such a crucial matter.

What amounted to a motion of no confidence in the Prime Minister was introduced in the House by Sir John Wardlaw-Milne, a Conservative and Chairman of the all-party Parliamentary Finance Committee. The real purpose of the motion was to take from Churchill's hands not so much the central direction of the war as the formulation of strategy, in which, as Minister of Defence, he had taken a large and sometimes over-riding hand and which it was felt should have been left to the Service Chiefs. But it can be safely assumed that if the motion had succeeded Churchill would have felt obliged to resign as Prime Minister.

At this stage of the war Britain had only a gloomy list of defeats to show for her efforts. In France, Norway, Greece, Crete, Hong Kong, Malaya, Burma and even, in early 1942, in North Africa our operations had led only to retreats and to failures. Our merchant fleet, too, had endured crippling losses.

To quote Lord Winterton in the ensuing debate, 'We never had anything in the last War comparable with this series of disasters.' The interests of national solidarity had long precluded public recrimination; but now it was felt that matters must be brought to a head.

As it happens, it was to be only a matter of a few weeks before the pendulum would begin to swing in the reverse direction and it would be the Axis powers who would suffer reverse after reverse. In Russia, North Africa, the Pacific and on the high seas generally the long haul to ultimate victory would have begun before the year ended. In June this could not be safely predicted, though there was every hope of it.

Such figures as Admiral of the Fleet Sir Roger Keyes, Aneurin Bevan and Leslie Hore-Belisha, a former Secretary of State for War, spoke in favour of the motion. Churchill looked harassed and everyone was emotional and uneasy. Wardlaw-Milne held the House well. He was fair, calm and dignified and he was listened to with respect until he made some strange suggestions; that Czech or Polish Generals be put in charge of our armies and that the Duke of Gloucester be made Commander-in-Chief of the Forces. The House roared with disrespectful laughter and Churchill knew that he was saved. Wardlaw-Milne never quite regained the hearing of the House.

Anxious moment. One of Lieutenant-Colonel Doolittle's Mitchells lifts off the carrier *Yorktown* (this was the second plane off).

Petty Officer Koga's Zero fighter as it was found by the Americans in the Aleutians.

After twenty-five years on the bottom. Floating Dock AFD 26 which sank with the *Valiant* in her.

In 1969 the author revisits the Officers' Mess and Quarters at China Bay. Time and neglect have completed the damage started by Japanese bombs.

When it was suggested that the Eastern Fleet had suffered a defeat at the hands of the Japanese, A. P. Herbert (Independent) made a very sound point in refutation. If you are attacked by a raging tiger, he claimed, and if when the onslaught is over you are still standing, you do not look on it as a defeat. The Eastern Fleet was still in being. That was something to be thankful for.

There were plenty of others to speak in Churchill's defence. His own oratory did the rest.

Though a small collection of abstainers remained silent on the benches, including Lady Violet Astor and Lady Megan Lloyd George, the motion was defeated by 475 votes to 25 and our solidarity was proclaimed afresh to the world.

The question inevitably arises: could we have taken a more positive line against the Japanese Fleet in April 1942? The loss of a single carrier would have made an enormous difference to Japan's ability to stand up to the United States in the Pacific. If Squadron Leader Ault's bombs had managed to sink Nagumo's flagship it would have been a triumphant finish to an otherwise ignominious chapter of the war. If the bombs had badly damaged her it is interesting to speculate what might have happened. Sir James Somerville and the fast section of the Eastern Fleet were miles away and virtually withdrawing from the theatre of operations. Would they have come back? It is more likely that the remainder of 11 Squadron's Blenheims would have been called to attack again and that the *Hermes'* Swordfish (814 Squadron, still at China Bay) would have been given the task of finishing off the *Akagi* with torpedoes. By daylight it would have been a perilous operation. By night it might have come off. The Japanese First Air Fleet could not have remained much longer so far from its bases and a crippled ship might have had to be abandoned or sunk.

Sir Winston Churchill, in *The Second World War* was disposed to the view that the air fighting over Ceylon had important strategic results which we could not foresee at the time. He wrote:

Admiral Nagumo's now celebrated carrier force, which had ranged almost unmolested for four months with devastating success, had on this occasion suffered such losses in the air that three of his ships had to be withdrawn to Japan to be refitted.

Thus when a month later Japan launched her attack against Port Moresby in New Guinea, only two of these carriers were able to take part. Their appearance at full strength then in the Coral Sea might well have turned the scale against the Americans in that important encounter.

It is certainly a fact that only the *Shokaku* and *Zuikaku* took part in the unsuccessful operations against New Guinea while the other three refitted in Japan. But it can scarcely be claimed with justification that air losses over Ceylon were the cause. If it had been so then our own heavy losses would not have been in vain.

What in fact were the Japanese losses? It is hard to say with any precision. The Japanese Imperial Headquarters issued a bulletin on the Colombo attack in which they stated they lost five planes. As far as can be traced no further bulletins were issued to cover the other operations. The best sources give seventeen aircraft as being lost over all the Ceylon operations (perhaps thirty men). This could possibly be a true figure though it is likely that only those lost to direct enemy action are included. Even suppose this figure were to be doubled, it would surely cover their overall losses.

Commander Eiziro Suzuki, who has given me some help with this book and who was a member of the Air Staff of the 2nd Flying Corps (in the carriers *Soryu* and *Hiryu*) during the Ceylon operations, does not even accept the figure of seventeen. 'I would like to say', he writes, 'that it was an exaggerated announcement of the British Navy that seventeen Japanese aeroplanes were damaged in this battle.'

Whatever the number, it seems to have been comparatively modest and this was the sum total of all Japanese material losses in the two weeks spent in the Indian Ocean in April 1942.

It is worthwhile calculating what they achieved at such modest cost. Our own losses were:

2 8″ cruisers with 425 men killed
1 aircraft carrier and 302 men killed
2 destroyers and 23 men (*Tenedos, Vampire*)
1 corvette and 4 men (estimated)
1 armed merchant cruiser and 4 men (estimated)

Casualties in the *Erebus* and *Lucia* – 10 killed (estimated)
23 merchant ships totalling 135,689 tons, mostly laden with
    cargo, and 90 men (estimated)
3 Catalina flying boats with 19 men killed (6 prisoners of war)
6 Swordfish torpedo-bombers and 5 men killed
7 Hurricane fighters and 12 pilots killed
5 Blenheim medium bombers and 17 men
6 Fulmar fleet fighters and 12 airmen
3 Men killed on the ground at China Bay
17 killed in the naval dockyard, Trincomalee
85 civilians killed in Colombo

Adding the civilians to the servicemen brings the total to 1028
lives lost.

These figures take no account of those wounded, nor of the
damage done to the two airfields, to Colombo Harbour workshops,
to various ships, to railway and oil installations and civilian
property. Nor do they include planes lost accidentally, otherwise
than by enemy action.

To the question, 'Could the Eastern Fleet have done more?' there
is a startlingly cynical answer. We would have fared much better
had we done far less. It cannot be seriously suggested that the
Eastern Fleet should have been given such orders but if they had
been told to keep out of the way and to stay in the Western Indian
Ocean, to which, in the event they were immediately withdrawn, or
if they had not even entered the Indian Ocean at all, the fruits of the
Japanese Navy's sorties would have been much more modest.
Admiral Ozawa's Malaya Force would have done no more and no
less than they actually did and the First Air Fleet would have had
deducted from their bag two cruisers and an aircraft carrier with its
attendant destroyer, which were their major successes.

This is, of course, being wise after the event; always a facile
operation. There would have been a terrible outcry if Admiral
Somerville had been told to stand clear of the battle from the start.
The country was sick by then of one withdrawal after another in
Asia. Yet these are the orders he ultimately received and there is
little doubt that the orders were wise. A prudent and, as yet,
ineffective Eastern Fleet in being was deemed of far greater value

than a courageous one at the bottom of the ocean. If they had lost a major naval engagement at this moment how could Britain have continued the struggle? We could not afford another Java Seas. This is the measure of Winston Churchill's gloom and apprehension and explains his enormous relief when Nagumo withdrew, with most of the British Eastern Fleet intact and Ceylon not invaded. His version of the events and the ultimate effect they had on the outcome of the war are understandably coloured by this relief.

It is now agreed that for all their easily won successes, the Japanese derived no significant strategic or tactical advantages from their naval operations in Ceylon waters. Indeed they may very well have squandered, though perhaps to a less extent than Churchill claims, valuable energy and resources which it would have paid them better to devote to the more crucial operations in the Pacific.

Had they wished to return to Ceylon with an invasion force, they could have landed almost unopposed. Our Fleet had retired; our air defences had been all but crippled. Essential civilian labour had fled from Colombo and, to a less extent, from Trincomalee, as was to happen from time to time at Calcutta in the coming months when sporadic bombing raids were made with just this object in view. In such conditions the military would have been sore put to it to defend the Island. The British Chiefs of Staff had dropped all pretence at disputing command of the sea and air in the Indian Ocean. It was frankly accepted that we were no longer in a position to defend Ceylon if the Japanese wished to press their advantage and to invade the Island. The Admiralty signalled Admiral Layton in mid-April that a full scale attack on Ceylon was now likely and there was no hope of immediate reinforcement in the area.

But there was to be no return of the Japanese. For the plans for actual invasion of Ceylon and Madagascar were rejected by the Japanese Imperial High Command. Both the Army and Navy Chiefs of Staff agreed that the time was unsuitable and that sufficient forces were not available. The idea in the end was never seriously considered. Far to the East they had, after all, already bitten off more than they would ever be allowed to digest. Further conquests were not out of the question.

To the world the Japanese had been repulsed for the first time since they had extended the war in Asia by their attack at Pearl Harbour. This much was known and, in spite of the apprehensions of the Chiefs of Staff, it caused rejoicing on a big scale. The effect on morale, at a time when we had few reasons for rejoicing, was out of all proportion to the actual situation, but was no less real for all that.

In Ceylon the elation that was felt at the stout defence put up in April 1942 was never to be effaced. When there was no return visit, no further westward incursion at all by the Japanese, the illusion of victory remained. Over the years it has even gained strength.

The illusion still remains. For the few who remember.

In July 1942 the Indian National Congress, pursuing its 'Quit India' movement, passed a long resolution which put their case to the World. One brief extract needs quoting:

> In making the proposal for the withdrawal of British rule from India, the Congress has no desire whatsoever to embarrass Great Britain or the Allied Powers in their prosecution of the War, or in any way to encourage aggression on India or increased pressure on China by the Japanese or any other Power associated with the Axis group.

The essential naivety of Gandhi's views was expressed in another statement which he made somewhat earlier, in May:

> The presence of the British in India is an invitation to Japan to invade India. Their withdrawal would remove the bait. Assume, however, that it does not. Free India would be better able to cope with the invasion. Unadulterated non-co-operation would then have full sway.

In the event *satyagraha* was pursued and from August 1942 onwards, after plans by the Congress Committee to welcome the Japanese had been found, Indian leaders were removed from the scene and again incarcerated for virtually the rest of the war.

Perhaps this term is too harsh, for Gandhi was held at the Aga Khan's palace at Poonah and Nehru at Ahmednagar Fort and the conditions of their retention were reasonably comfortable. The step was much deplored in America and elsewhere but was considered necessary for the preservation of good order. With their departure dissolved such goodwill as had survived the struggle and all prospect of India's masses becoming wholeheartedly involved in the war.

Across the frontier, behind the Japanese occupiers of Burma, a new figure now loomed up as a potential leader of Indian nationalism, the way smoothed by the repression of India's recognised leaders.

Some 60,000 Indian members of the Armed Forces had fallen into enemy hands when Singapore, Malaya and Burma were lost. To the Japanese they seemed fruitful material for the spread of their Greater East Asia Co-prosperity Sphere. An organisation known as the Indian National Army was formed, its leader Subhas Chandra Bose, a Cambridge graduate who had led the more radical element of the Indian National Congress and been elected its President in 1938–9.

Bose went further. In July 1943 he set up a 'Provisional Government of India' with himself as President and three months later formally declared war on Britain and the United States. The Japanese organised a Free India Radio for him and broadcasts were regularly made to India. Mahatma Gandhi's name was freely used (Gandhi himself being, of course, in internment) and there is no doubt that the broadcasts had considerable appeal to listeners in India, though in the 1940's this would have constituted only a small proportion of the populace. The writer has been surprised how often were to be seen, a quarter of a century after his death, photographs of Subhas Chandra Bose in the bazaars of both India and Ceylon. His portrait figures almost as frequently as those of Mahatma Gandhi and Pandit Nehru. Gandhi himself played an important part in building up a somewhat idealised picture of Bose as a self-sacrificing, peaceful nationalist. In fact it is likely he would have tried to establish an iron dictatorship over India with Japanese help, a policy which would have been much at variance with Gandhi's ideas of *ahimsa*.

Considering the appalling neglect and harsh conditions meted out by the Japanese to their war prisoners, it is to be wondered that no more than a third of captive Indian nationals were persuaded to join. Kept mainly in reserve the Japanese dared place no great reliance on an army arrayed against its homeland, even in the guise of liberators. When peace came at last, ex-INA members were an embarrassment to India. After some heart searching the authorities fortunately decided on leniency. No strong action was taken against INA members although some were briefly imprisoned.

'Netaji' (the Leader), as Bose became popularly known, would have proved a far greater embarrassment than the rank and file he had recruited. To have treated 'Free India's' fiery head of state as a war criminal would assuredly have raised a hornet's nest.

Providence, however, decreed his death in a plane crash in Formosa just as the war in Asia ended.

One of the minor dramas to be played out in the Indian Ocean a year after the operations we have been considering was the trans-shipment in mid-ocean of Chandra Bose from the German submarine *U–180* to the Japanese *I–29* after a sojourn in Berlin. He had to spend three uncomfortable months in the submarines, was often seasick and on one occasion had to be retrieved from overboard. En route he was a mute witness to the sinking of the Shell tanker *Corbus*, some 500 miles south-east of Durban.

In the event the Japanese, challenged, checked and ultimately held by the throat by the Americans in the Pacific, never progressed beyond the Indian frontier. Their sole attempt, heralded on Free-India Radio as an all-out assault with New Delhi as its objective (and for some time taken to be such by Indian listeners) progressed no further than Kohima and Imphal, barely on Indian soil, and cost the Japanese so dearly in men that from then onwards Burma could no longer be effectively held.

It only took the horror of the atomic bombs dropped on Hiroshima and Nagasaki to point to the futility of the whole campaign in Burma, as futile for the British as for the Japanese. Burma itself, rising from the ravages of the war to a troubled independence, was to be equally lost to both sides.

In Ceylon the four detainees who had escaped from the Kandy military gaol during the April raids remained undetected in hiding for some time and Leslie Goonewardena, Secretary of the Lanka Samasamaja Party, continued to avoid arrest altogether. Although the party had been proclaimed illegal, its members managed to have clandestinely printed a pamphlet 'From the Workers and Peasants of Ceylon' for distribution to Allied troops. The Pamphlet, dated 20th April 1942, is reproduced in Appendix 'A'. Bracketing Churchill with Hitler and Tojo as bloodthirsty exploiters, and heavily larded with the time-worn, humourless clichés of the Communist propagandist, the pamphlet exhorted troops to take matters into their own hands 'seeing that you are many and your officers are few'. Needless to say such appeals fell on entirely deaf ears and the pamphlet caused only a certain amount of amusement.

One of the escapees, Edmund Samarakoddy, elected to remain in Ceylon, which he must have regretted, for he was tracked down and re-arrested, but the others, including Leslie Goonewardena, moved undetected to India where party members had taken refuge when the LSSP had been earlier proscribed. Allying themselves with the Bolshevik Leninist Party of India Burma and Ceylon (Fourth International) they took some part in the disturbances which, as we have seen, led to the re-arrest of the Indian Leaders in August. These activities, however, brought them to the notice of the Indian Police and Philip Gunewardena and Dr N. M. Perera were extradited and returned to detention in Ceylon for the rest of the War. Dr Colvin de Silva, however, successfully evaded arrest and did not return to Ceylon until the war was over when the LSSP was again legalised and formed the main opposition to Mr D. S. Senanayake's first government in the Independent Dominion of Ceylon.

Until very recently (1975) Dr N. M. Perera has been Minister of Finance, Mr Leslie Goonewardena Minister of Communications and Dr Colvin R. de Silva Minister of Plantation Industry and of Constitutional Affairs.

On the anniversary of the Easter Sunday raid on Colombo, on 5th April 1971, a serious revolution broke out in Ceylon. Undoubtedly Communist inspired, it is ironical that this should have been levied against a government containing so many ministers of the same (or at any rate similar) political persuasion.

The British Eastern Fleet made its return to Ceylon waters on 4th September 1943, when its Headquarters moved once again to

Colombo. By that time it was scarcely recognisable as the Fleet which had retreated to the African coast eighteen months before. Urgent needs in other more active, and in the changing circumstances more important, theatres of war had whittled away all of the larger ships and no aircraft carriers or battleships could at first be spared. Later the *Queen Elizabeth* and the *Valiant* formed the nucleus at Trincomalee.

Both these battleships had been put out of action at Alexandria by Italian limpet mines earlier on in the war and the *Valiant* was to come to grief again in Trinco harbour when a newly constructed floating dock, AFD 26, reputed to be the biggest ever built and one of a pair towed round from Bombay where they had been built and equipped with American machinery, broke its back in spectacular fashion with the *Valiant* berthed in her. The battleship's bows were soon poised well above the water line, with her stern submerged, and to save the *Valiant* from breaking her own back drastic measures had to be taken. Depth charges were dropped to settle the dock on an even keel. As it was, the *Valiant* was so badly damaged that she had to return to Britain on one screw for repairs and took no further active part in the war. The dock itself, part of whose twisted superstructure protruded from the harbour waters for the best part of twenty five years, was raised in 1968, after numerous others had failed, by a team of French divers headed by Mr Victor Baroukh of Produits Metallurgiques. Amongst those who had tried and failed was a Japanese syndicate.

Admiral Somerville retained command of the Fleet long enough to see it take offensive action against Sabaing and Palembang where oil and other installations were bombed. He then handed over to Admiral Sir Bruce Fraser. Later, when the British Pacific Fleet was formed and made a brief appearance in support of the Americans as they finally closed in on Japan, both the *Formidable* and *Indomitable* were there. Each was struck by Kamikaze suicide bombers, though their steel decks managed to withstand the shock with only mild indentations to show for it.

The *Warspite, Erebus* and the 4 Rs all took part in landings or bombardments on D-Day, at Walcheren, in the South of France and elsewhere and all survived the war, to finish in the shipbreakers' yard.

In marked contrast, the entire complement of Vice-Admiral Nagumo's fleet, taking all units from light cruisers upwards, were to face destruction before hostilities were over. The Americans would see to that.

We have seen that within two months of the Trincomalee raid, three out of the five carriers had been sent to the bottom in the Battle of Midway. The *Shokaku,* after being severely damaged in the Battle of the Coral Sea, was sunk by the US submarine *Carvalla* on 19th June 1944 in the extended operations known collectively as The Battle of the Philippine Sea and the *Zuikaku,* damaged in this same battle, was finished off by bombing in the Battle of Leyte Gulf on 25th October 1944. The cruisers *Chikuma* and *Abukama* were lost with her. The four battleships fared no better. The *Hiei* and *Kirishima* were sunk off Guadalcanal on 13th November 1942 and the American submarine *Sea Lion* torpedoed the *Kongo* just two years later. Last of all, the *Haruna* was blasted to destruction by American bombers at the naval base of Kure during the last month of the war.

Ozawa's ships, too, were not destined to survive for long. His light carrier the *Ryujo* was sunk off the Solomon Islands on 24th August 1942 and three of his cruisers were amongst the heavy losses inflicted on the Japanese at Leyte Gulf.

When the ominous news reached Japan that a heavy American attack was developing on Okinawa, probably the last island stepping stone before the Japanese mainland itself would be assaulted and a base from which heavy bombing must be expected if it passed into American hands, Admiral Soemi Toyoda, who had succeeded to the overall command of the Imperial Fleet when Admiral Yamamoto had been shot down and killed, was faced with the task of interfering as best he could with the American operations.

All that could be got together for the task was the huge, 63,000 ton *Yamato,* the cruiser *Yahagi* and eight destroyers. Toyoda had the greatest difficulty in raising the necessary fuel but they sailed from the Inland Sea on 5th April 1945. It was the third anniversary of the Colombo raid.

In spite of the lessons which had been learnt, the force sailed entirely without air cover. By this stage none could be provided.

Their mission was just as suicidal as those of the kamikaze bombers who were by then causing such havoc amongst American warships in the Pacific theatre. The *Yamato* and *Yahagi* would now be exposed to the same risks as the *Prince of Wales* and *Repulse* had been.

By the 7th, American bombers, with some assistance from submarines, had sent the whole force to the bottom except for four destroyers which, left with nothing to escort, managed to escape northwards.

Amongst the lost destroyers was the *Isokaze* (Surf Wind) now under the captainship of Commander Saneo Maeda, which had fished the 413 Squadron survivors from the sea three years before. She had been present at Pearl Harbour, the first operation against the American Navy, had done much else besides, including the rescue of many survivors from the sinking carrier *Zuikaku* in the Battle of Leyte Gulf and had now met her end in what was virtually the last surface operation against American forces. For the action north of Okinawa finally put paid to Japanese sea power in World War II. Only her submarines were still able to operate effectively.

Admiral Ishizaki's flotilla which had done so well along the East African coast had fared no better, however, than the surface forces of Admirals Nagumo and Ozawa. By July 1944 three of his submarines had fallen to American destroyers; the other two had disappeared from the scene for uncertain causes.

No major Japanese forces entered the Indian Ocean again, with the exception of a brief foray between the Cocos Islands and Australia by the heavy cruisers *Tone, Chikuma* and *Aoba* in March 1944. Vice-Admiral Naomosa Sakonju commanded this force and his orders were to disrupt Allied shipping lines and to capture Allied shipping.

When they found the British motor vessel *Behar* (7,840 tons) in the neighbourhood of the Cocos Islands and failed to get her to stop she was shelled and sunk. Passengers and crew numbered one hundred and eleven. All but three who had been killed in the shelling took to the boats. Somewhat inexplicably, all were taken on board the *Tone*. Captain Mayazumi, who commanded the cruiser, seems to have shown some humanity here, but he was ill rewarded. Admiral Sakonju ordered him to 'dispose of' all but a few.

The squadron put in at Batavia with the Admiral's orders still not carried out. Here thirty-six survivors were landed, leaving seventy-two still in custody on board the *Tone*. To his credit Mayazumi did his best to persuade the Admiral to countermand his order for their slaughter. In this he failed and when they put to sea again he could only pass on the order to his subordinates. All the prisoners were bludgeoned or hacked to death and thrown overboard.

At a subsequent War Crimes trial Admiral Sakonju was, not surprisingly, setenced to death. Captain Mayazumi, accused of the same crime and, in common with all war criminals, alike in Asia as in Europe, denied the right to plead that he was carrying out the orders of a superior, was sentenced to seven years imprisonment.

Another engagement deserves to be mentioned. This took place in a remote sector of the Indian Ocean and Japanese forces for once fared unexpectedly badly. It was 11th November 1942, another anniversary. This time it was of the signing of the Armistice which ended World War I.

Some 1,500 miles west of Freemantle, from which she had sailed, the Dutch tanker *Ondina* (6,341 tons) (Captain H. Wildman) was proceeding north-westwards, escorted only by the 650 ton Royal Indian Navy minesweeper *Bengal* (Lieutenant- Commander W. J. Wilson, RINR) when, at first light, two large merchant vessels were sighted which closed them and opened fire with armament of a range, intensity and calibre which made it clear that these were no ordinary merchantmen.

The *Bengal* interposed herself between the *Ondina* and the raiders (as they were now recognised to be) and replied with her single 12-pounder gun. Her intention was to attract the enemy's fire while the *Ondina* escaped. But the tanker's Dutch Master did no such thing. Instead he joined in the battle with his single 4-inch gun.

Both the *Ondina* and the *Bengal* continued to fire until their ammunition was expended. By this time a heavy explosion had been seen on one of the raiders, which then sank, and the other had retired after picking up survivors.

The *Ondina,* however, was on fire and several of her crew, including her spirited Captain, had been killed. The survivors abandoned ship.

The second raider re-appeared, machine gunned the boats somewhat half-heartedly, without hitting them, and then disappeared again. When it was realised that she had gone for good and when the fire on the *Ondina* was seen to be getting no worse she was re-boarded and in the end managed to return under her own steam to Fremantle.

The *Bengal,* too, reached Diego Garcia safely.

We now know that the Japanese raider which they had sunk was the *Hokaku Maru,* which had succoured the 1st Division of the Japanese 8th Submarine Flotilla in their operations in the Western Indian Ocean in May and June. The identity of the other raider is uncertain, though it seems highly probable that she would have been the *Aikoku Maru.*

Though major Japanese warships were not to be active again in the Indian Ocean, their submarines continued to be spasmodically active. One of their more notable sinkings was of the troopship *Khedive Ismail* which sank in a matter of a few minutes with very heavy loss of life, including a detachment of Nursing Sisters.

Oddly enough, in spite of their many pre-occupations in other theatres and in spite of the enormous distances involved, almost as much was done in this sphere by German U-Boats, refuelled and succoured by disguised depot ships in the remotest southern oceans or by the Japanese at Penang and Batavia, where the same distant and chilly co-operation prevailed between Japanese and Germans as did between the British and Russians over the Arctic convoys.

British and Dutch submarines also played their part over the ensuing years, operating from Ceylon and scoring a steady succession of useful sinkings of enemy ships, mainly in the Straits of Malacca.

Though Ceylon was not to be threatened again by Japanese surface forces, a few aircraft were to make an appearance over the island later. These were Kawanishi, Type 1 Flying-boats (Emilys), huge 4-engined planes which, when Japanese intelligence must have had word, quite correctly, that the Eastern Fleet was returning to Ceylon waters, were flown on full moon nights to Colombo and Trincomalee, seeking confirmation. One dropped a few bombs harmlessly on the East coast. The flights were far too regular for their own good. By then Ceylon had a small flight of radar-equipped Beaufighters and these stood by at the time of the full moon to deal with them. Two Emilys were shot down, one of them off Trincomalee and one off Colombo. There were no survivors, though some bodies were recovered from the sea.

It is clear that the Japanese expected radar-equipped fighters, for they dropped a certain amount of 'window', the tin foil strips which, fluttering in clusters in the night air, were designed to distract the radar operators. Even so they proved rather sitting ducks.

At this time a message was received at the RAF station at China Bay from a village headman to the effect that the remains of a plane had been found in remote jungle some miles south of Koddiar Bay. A party was organised to visit the scene in the hope that it was another enemy flying-boat, but it proved to be one of the Fulmars missing from the Trincomalee attack eighteen months before, and what little remained of its pilot and observer.

Several of the RAF Squadrons of 222 Group, Ceylon, moved on at one stage or another to Burma. Flight Lieutenant D. J. T. Sharp, the New Zealander who led a flight of Hurricanes of 258 Squadron in the Easter Sunday raid, later commanded No 11 Squadron in Burma. By then they had relinquished their Blenheims and were flying Hurricane attack bombers, and later American-built Vengeances. He had a gruelling time accompanying Wingate and his Chindits (this time on foot) on their first expedition as Air Liaison Officer. Furthermore he was selected by Bernard Fergusson as leader of one of the three parties into which the Force was split when, after suffering heavy casualties, they had to fight their way back to India.

Squadron Leader Birchall had a further role to play before the war was ended. After surviving six months with two of his companions (three others were separated for hospitalisation) at a special interrogation camp at Ojuna, where starvation diet and constant beatings were their lot, he was moved to a work camp near Yokohama. Here he was Senior Allied Officer amongst some 350 prisoners of war. There were British from Hong Kong and elsewhere, Americans from the Philippines and other nationalities from Wake, Singapore and Allied ships. Miserably underfed, deprived of medical supplies, they were required to work 12 hours a day and were always liable to be beaten up at the whim of their guards.

Here, and later at the Osano dock camp, Birchall strove courageously for reasonable treatment for the prisoners, particularly those who were too sick to work. On one occasion he physically fought a Japanese sergeant named Ushida who had beaten a man too weak to work.

'Once I started slugging him,' says Birchall, 'I knew I might just as well finish the job.' When in recognition he was awarded the OBE, the citation stated:

> On many occasions with complete disregard for his own safety Squadron Leader Birchall prevented, as far as possible, Japanese officials from sadistically beating his men and denying prisoners the medical treatment which they urgently needed. Birchall forcibly intervened on behalf of his men in the full knowledge that he would receive brutal treatment. The consistant gallantry and devotion to his fellow prisoners of war that this officer displayed throughout his lengthy period of imprisonment are in keeping with the finest traditions of the Royal Canadian Air Force.

When the time came for the Japanese War Crimes Trials, Squadron Leader Birchall was an important witness in several cases, including Sergeant Ushida's, and was to re-visit Ceylon on his return from the trials. In 1967, by which time he was an Air Commodore Commanding the Royal Military College of Canada, he returned to the Island as a guest of the Ceylon Government in connection with Canada's Centenary Celebrations.

Of his crew, one, Brian Catlin, found himself back in Ceylon after the War when he was stationed briefly at Koggala. He rose later to the rank of Squadron Leader in the RAF by which time he had developed ties of a closer kind to his fellow crew member and prisoner of war, Sergeant Bill Cook, who had been badly hurt when their Catalina was attacked. After the war in New Zealand Cook had to endure the amputation of his shattered leg and married the girl who nursed him. Catlin later married her sister in England.

Cook died recently. The war had left its mark on him in more ways than one. It was a topic he was never prepared to discuss.

Another 413 Squadron airman to remain on in the Service after the war and to reach commissioned rank was 'Bart' Onyette, Birchall's navigator, now a wing commander in the RCAF.

Apart from the Ceylonese (Bugler McLeod was retired a few years ago as a Company Sergeant Major in the Ceylon Army) none of the Europeans involved in the Indian Ocean Operations remain in Ceylon to-day. John Loam, who flew a Blenheim in one of the abortive strikes, and Roy Hinton of 803 Squadron, Fleet Air Arm, who both settled in Ceylon after the war years, were probably the last to go in the late sixties. Sir John Kotelawala, now living in Kent, is only an infrequent visitor to Ceylon these days.

The *bhikku* beside whose temple Squadron Leader Fletcher fell dramatically from the skies on Easter Sunday received an unusual presentation from the hands of the Duke of Gloucester when he visited Ceylon a few weeks after the raid. When the Zero began its dive on Fletcher, the priest claimed, he swiftly covered the airman with his saffron robe and the Japanese, a Buddhist of course, did not fire. Though Air Chief Marshal Sir Peter Fletcher (as he now is) says the story is apocryphal, it is understandable that the *bhikku* will have believed that his robes, clearly visible as they must have been, will have been the means of saving a British airman's life. His bravery and presence of mind were thus recorded on a presentation plaque, handed to him by the Duke.

Air Marshal Sir John d'Albiac, before his death, became a familiar figure as Officer Commanding London Airport at Heathrow, where his duties included the official welcoming of visiting dignitaries.

The two fighter pilots decorated for their deeds over Colombo on Easter Sunday went their separate ways. Teddy Peacock-Edwards, after leaving the RAF, rejoined the peace-time service (in which his son has followed him) and is now in business in Durban. Squadron Leader Fletcher has only recently retired from the Service, having finished up as Vice-Chief of Air Staff.

Lieutenant Longsdon, who found himself upside down in a paddy field, with severe face wounds, on Easter Sunday morning, moved, like Flight Lieutenant Hildyard, into the diplomatic sphere after the War. When last contacted he was British Consul at Split, in Jugo Slavia.

Others in the Cape Province of South Africa, where this book has been written, are two *Cornwall* survivors, Commander John Milner and Commander Geoffrey Grove; Ray Lock of the *Dorsetshire* and Dennis Brimble, who was Second Gunnery Officer in the *Hermes*. Grove had to endure a second sinking in a troopship in the Mediterranean.

Captain Agar of the *Dorsetshire* retired to Alton, Hampshire, where he died early in 1969. Captain Manwaring, who commanded the *Cornwall* is also now dead.

Admiral Somerville, allowed to return once more to the retirement from which he had been unwillingly recalled, became Lord Lieutenant of Somerset (a pity it could not have been Dorsetshire or even Cornwall!) but died in 1949.

Of the Japanese who fought in April 1942 there are few who lived on into peacetime. Fuchida was one. He owes his survival largely to the fact that he developed appendicitis on the way to Midway, was operated on immediately by the *Akagi*'s surgeon (cared for no doubt by the same staff who had tended the RAF prisoners) and was still recuperating when the Battle that Doomed Japan, to use his own phrase, was fought. He was able, though still weak and shakey, to witness it all at first hand. When attacks by American Dauntless dive-bombers left the *Akagi* crippled and sinking, he was taken off with Admiral Nagumo by the light cruiser *Nagaro* and had the misfortune, on top of all his other difficulties, to break both ankles in the jump. After Midway he became an instructor at the Naval War College and later Air Operations Officer at Combined Fleet Headquarters. His son and daughter are now, strangely enough, American citizens and he himself, an ardent convert to Christianity, at one time contemplated following their example.

And what of Nagumo?

On 9th July 1944, as American marines completed the occupation of Saipan in the Marianas against fanatical last-ditch Japanese opposition, Vice-Admiral Chuichi Nagumo put a pistol to his head and took his own life, with numerous others of his staff following his example. His body was unrecognised amongst the others but the evidence is clear enough.

When it had been suggested that Nagumo should be relieved of his command for an alleged partial failure at Pearl Harbour, Admiral Yamamoto who was until his death in 1944, when his plane was shot down by American fighters, Commander-in-Chief of the Japanese Combined Fleet, had described Chuichi Nagumo as 'an old fashioned Samurai type. If I move him he will commit hara-kiri because he will consider it such a disgrace'.

Yamamoto obviously knew his man.

Thus in a remote cave (some accounts say in a hut) perished obscurely the proud commander of the Japanese First Air Fleet which had struck the first crucial blow against Pearl Harbour and had ranged victoriously as far east as Honolulu and as far west as Ceylon.

Fuchida speaks of Admiral Nagumo with a noticeable lack of enthusiasm and considers him to have been a square peg in a round hole as C-in-C First Air Fleet. He implies that, aware of his increasing age, he seldom took the initiative and generally did little more than approve the recommendations of his staff.

Be this as it may, his enormous success at Pearl Harbour and for the ensuing six months of early 1942 cannot be gainsaid. Although he met with ultimate disaster he must be allowed his place amongst that small but select band, the Admirals of World War II who profoundly influenced events.

Admiral Ozawa succeeded Nagumo in the command of what was left of the First Air Fleet. He was another of the few Japanese naval officers to live on until after the War.

Commander Shigeru Itaya who led the fighters, both at Pearl Harbour and in the Ceylon operations, was killed in 1944, and so was Captain Takashige Egusa.

The airfield at Ratmalana has changed little since the war. A few modern hangars have gone up and the surrounding coconut plantations are slowly giving way to warehouses and factories which, under Ceylon's modest industrialisation policy, are being sited in the district. Even Sir John Kotelawala's house, 'Kandawela', is much as it was. The lagoon at Koggala has returned to its accustomed quietude. The war might never have touched the place for all that can be seen there to-day.

The Racecourse strip did not long survive the war. The Turf Club resumed possession for a decade or so until, largely on religious grounds, racing became proscribed. An Industrial Exhibition was held in its grounds, some of whose buildings remain, and the grandstand has been commandeered as a somewhat incongruous wing of Ceylon's University.

With the small Ceylon Air Force in occupation, there is remarkably little change to be seen at China Bay Airfield. In August 1944 the 30th US Army Air Corps, flying new B29 Super-fortresses, flew a single operation from this station, moving in for a few days from their normal base in Assam and swamping and far outnumbering the small resident RAF contingent. Oil installations at Palembang were their target. For some months much hasty preparatory work had been done, enlarging the runway by an extra 1,000 yards, necessary for these enormous long-range bombers. Results, we now know, scarcely justified the enormous effort expended on the raid which was never repeated from Ceylon.

Early in 1945 when VE Day in Europe loomed up and preparations were being made for the final struggle against Japan, enormous extensions by way of additional hangars, widely dispersed off the aerodrome itself, and new personnel camps were being built at China Bay, by then in the hands of the Fleet Air Arm. Most of these were in the direction of Clappenberg Bay. They were never used for warlike purposes. To-day the hangars fortuitously house the large imported grain stocks which, in spite of the ever-increasing home production of rice, must still be shipped in.

Trincomalee harbour, in spite of its wonderful potentialities, is never used to anything like its capacity in marked contrast to Colombo's cramped artificial harbour on the opposite coast, though most of Ceylon's tea is shipped here.

To-day only cement foundations, overgrown with vegetation or half covered with sand and scrub, betray the sites of camps which once housed Askaris, training for the Burma campaign, Cochin and Malayalam Labour Units, an Indian Air Force Balloon Squadron, a hush-hush 'cloak and dagger' unit, Service Corps, Ordinance Depots and even latterly Wrens. It takes all sorts to wage a war.

Only the fishing villages are unchanged.

Fishermen from the villages on Ceylon's East Coast will tell you (for she teems with fish) that on clear, still, aquamarine days, when the surface of the sea is like glass, the dark shape of the *Hermes* can still be perceived on the sea bottom, some thirty fathoms down. Quite recently an American, Peter Gimbel, with Rodney Jonklaas, well known in Ceylon for his under-water exploits, have ventured down into the depths and brought back a few shots of the *Hermes* in her murky grave for the film *Blue Water, White Death.*

Captain Agar, feeling this was akin to desecrating a grave, voiced mild disapproval but His Honour Commander L. K. A. Block (who has an unusual combination of courtesy title and rank as a retired naval officer and judge of the City of London Court), the senior surviving officer from the *Hermes,* was able to take a more practical view. He had even hoped that his gold cigarette case might be recovered from his cabin on the bridge. Alas, this could not be managed.

But the *Dorsetshire* and *Cornwall,* with the men who went down in them, are where no mortal eye will see them again, fathoms down, in seas which will always remain comparatively remote and untenanted.

Though nearly all the servicemen who gave their lives were lost at sea with no known resting place, a few grave stones once stood, walled off in their own shady secluded corner of Kannatte, Colombo's main cemetery, where Japanese airmen who had crashed during the Easter Sunday raid were buried and one at least from the flying boat, shot down later. But soon after the war their remains were removed to be re-interred, with due honour and ceremony, in their own country. Hard by Allied servicemen who died at the same time are interred. A few of the *Hermes'* crew; those who survived the sinking but died later of their wounds; sailors from the *Tenedos,* and the airmen from all over the Commonwealth who fought and died over Colombo. Few who pass by their grave stones today know of their significance. Which is not so surprising. For they died a whole generation ago, birds of passage, most of them very much strangers in a distant land, not knowing Ceylon at all well even though they died in the Island's defence.

The same can be said for those whose remains lie in a small military cemetery beside the coastal road a few miles north of Trincomalee. It is a peaceful place, but still kept very trim by a resident attendant. The War Graves Commission have not ceased to make periodical visits; but they have been after all (at any rate until very recently) still tending the graves of British sailors lost long ago in the Napoleonic wars, graves which are hidden amongst the jungle growth on lonely Sober Island, just outside Trincomalee Harbour.

It is hard in the telling to bring home the reality of the snuffing out of so many lives in one fell swoop or to avoid the appearance of recounting their numbers in the dispassionate tones of a radio announcer giving out cricket scores. Yet almost all were very young men, scarcely on the threshold of adult life, drawn only recently, most of them, from every walk of civilian life, and leaving behind them twice, perhaps three times, their number in bereaved dependents and relations who must endure, many of them, profound disruption in their living arrangements for the rest of their days. And death must often have brought its terrors and been anguished and slow in coming. It is only in the Hollywood 'Western' that all the casualties conveniently drop, instantly dead from mortal bullet wounds. In reality men cling more tenaciously to life; most injuries are not fatal and those that are may take their time to lay their victims low.

These young men had to make their enormous sacrifice uncheered by the knowledge that their deaths would, in the end, help to earn us ultimate victory.

If by some joyous dispensation, some splendid superhuman process, they could be transported to life again over the intervening distances of time and space to look upon the world as it has since evolved, it is a sad reflection that they might be hard put to it, from what would confront them to-day, to determine whether their war had been won or lost.

In Asia, as in Europe, the Allies who fought together in World War II are now disrupted. Former enemies have been welcomed into the fold and old comrades are now aligned against us. The British Commonwealth has virtually dissolved and (something which would have surely shocked them with its resulting problems of divided loyalties) there is even disharmony amongst its hard core of white, basically British-descended, members as well as amongst Africans and Asiatics. A strangely different China is a great power to be reckoned with and not merely a lame duck to be bolstered up by Western arms. There are no Japanese-held provinces, it is true, and few Japanese are conspicuous elsewhere in Asia, though their staggering industrial growth and resulting influence might, to a war casualty back from the grave, seem to gainsay a total Japanese defeat. So would the raw materials which now find their way to Japan, much of it from Asian lands from which British, Dutch and French interests have wholly withdrawn.

India, its off-shoot Pakistan, Burma, Malaya and what had been formerly called collectively the Dutch East Indies are independent. But the liberation of subject peoples was, after all, one of our proclaimed war aims, however equivocal the term might have seemed where colonialism had prevailed. Viet Nam would surely cause some head scratching, though of white troops there are now none to be found in any other Eastern theatre.

One of the last bases to survive in British hands in Asia was Gan, the largest of the coral islands which surround the lagoon at Addu Atoll. When the Maldives became independent in 1965 an agreement was signed reserving the right to use for 20 years this remote staging-post, lying conveniently in the very centre of the Indian Ocean. Even this, however, is to be relinquished, for the concept no longer fits in with Britain's defence plans. The United States, however, have deemed fit to plan a base at Diego Garcia in the Chagos Archipelago.

In Ceylon the reins of office are to a large extent in the hands of the very leftist dissidents who were interned in 1942.

If those young service men were to be rewarded with a brief glimpse of the world from which they had been so cruelly torn we could hardly blame them were they to ask, 'But was it all worth it?' They would surely take the view that their deaths had been in vain; that we had failed to stem the tide flooding westwards from Japan; that we had lost all influence in Asia.

For, after devoting her energies to economic matters and making a quite phenomenal recovery from the appalling ravages in material destruction and loss of manpower which she endured during the war, Japan is again free to arm, with the full sanction of America and the West. Her eyes are turned not only in the direction which brought her to destruction in 1945, westwards to Asia, but even beyond. In the vastly changed conditions of to-day perhaps, in the end, her economic weapons are all she will need to accomplish her aims.

Since Japan is now aligned against Communism we shall not hinder her this time. We may even encourage her.

Epilogue – Part Two

Extract from a letter from Mr Lester Pearson, then Prime Minister of Canada, to Air Commodore Birchall:

Sir Winston went on very dramatically to say that this unknown airman, who lay deep in the waters of the Indian Ocean, made one of the most important single contributions to victory. He got quite emotional about it.

I broke in to tell him that the 'unknown airman' was not lying deep in the Indian Ocean but was an officer in the Royal Canadian Air Force, stationed down the street from the British Embassy where he was active in our military mission. I gather I was not quite accurate in this, as you were not in Washington at the time, but I hope I will be forgiven.

Mr Churchill was surprised and delighted to know that the end of the story was a happier one than he had envisaged.

Appendix A

(Text of a pamphlet distributed to British troops in Ceylon in April 1942)

A MESSAGE FROM THE WORKERS AND PEASANTS OF CEYLON

Comrades in the Army, Navy and Air Force,

The Workers and Peasants of Ceylon extend to you their warmest Revolutionary Greetings! You have gone through the Hell of Dunkirk and Singapore and have been dragged through the mire of Norway, Crete, Libya and Malaya by your High Command. You have been mercilessly exposed to the terrible dangers of land, sea and air attack and have seen the blood of thousands of your brother soldiers and sailors spilled on strange seas and lands that you have never known. 90,000 of your brothers have been sacrificed at Singapore by your heartless High Command. And now you have been brought to this island of Ceylon far, far away from your own country and your homes, to lay down your lives for what your rulers call 'Freedom'. What freedom did you British workers enjoy at home? Did you not ask for bread and employment, for better conditions of work and higher wages? And what did you get? The reply of your bosses to this demand of yours was *this war*. This war in which *you* have been conscripted to sacrifice *your lives* in the interests of your oppressors and exploiters at home. The Churchills, the Beaverbrooks, the Manchester Mill Owners, the Sheffield Steel and Armament Kings and the Metropolitan Vickers Combine. These *exploiters* and *warmongers,* the National Government and the Capitalists, with the help of their lackeys and boot lickers, the Trade Union Bureaucrats, the Citrines and the Bevins, the Labour Party Bosses, the Attlees and Greenwoods, as well as the C. P. agents of Stalin, the Gallachers and Pollitts, are *deceiving* you. Their whole propaganda machine labours to make you believe that this is a war for democracy against fascism, for civilisation against barbarism. Have you forgotten that this was the same story with which your fathers were deceived during the last war into fighting the battle of their capitalist bosses? Surely you will not allow yourselves to be fooled as your fathers were fooled. They thought that they were fighting for civilisation, that is for peace, employment and better conditions of life. You know what they got, *Hunger, Slums, Unemployment,* Crisis after Crisis, and now this murderous *Imperialist war.* So long as you are ruled by the National Government of Capitalists and Profiteers, so long as these Capitalists and Profiteers *own* your factories and work places, so long as you place your trust in their despicable agents, the Attlees, Citrines, Bevins, Pollitts and other Labour Bureaucrats, so long must you expect to suffer the *fate of your fathers.* Your real enemies are these parasites. These parasites are our enemies as well. This war, we have said, is *not your war. It is not our war too.* You will have noticed the effects of the first air raid on Colombo. You know how the workers ran away from the workshops and the City and its suburbs. The shops, hotels, laundries and barber saloons have closed down. The train and bus services have been disorganised. The normal life of the city has been brought to a standstill. *Why?* Have you not asked yourselves *why* this has happened in Malaya, Singapore, Burma and India too? You have been brought all this way to die defending Ceylon when the Ceylonese masses themselves *refuse to lift a finger* in its defence. This is easily explained. We are not interested in the defence of a country *which does not belong to us.* This country does not belong to you either. It belongs to the Imperialist bosses who exploit us here just as they exploit you at home. *They are our common enemies.* It is a shameless lie of the Imperialists that this war is being fought for Democracy and Freedom because every worker in India and Ceylon knows that there is *not a trace* of democracy in these countries but a *monstrous fascist regime* which has muzzled the Press, destroyed freedom of speech, attacked strikes and workers' meetings with armed police, *shot down* workers on strike, thrown Trade Union leaders into gaol *without trial,* illegalised working class parties and incarcerated their leaders.

You in the Army, Navy and Air Force are not free from oppression. You know that you are badly equipped, badly paid, badly fed, badly clothed, badly housed. Your officers on the other hand enjoy comforts and privileges which are denied to you who face the greatest dangers. Will you be deceived by them? And by the Society women who fawn on you now but will shun you like the plague once the war is over and *their ends* have been served? Or will you not rather, seeing that you are *many* and your officers are *few,* seize this opportunity to end oppression and secure your rights and liberties? In this struggle against the same Wavells and Laytons who exploit us, we promise you our wholehearted support.

We want to tell you soldier and sailor comrades that *British Imperialism cannot survive in India and Ceylon* because the *hundreds of millions* of workers and peasants of these two countries are *opposed* to the war effort of their exploited Government. In India and Ceylon thousands of you soldiers will be compelled to make another of those very 'strategic retreats' which mean the tragic slaughter of thousands of lives in a vain and murderous struggle.

But our opposition to the war of the British Imperialists against Japan and Germany does not mean that we intend to welcome the armies of the Mikado with open arms. *We are not the fifth columnists of any imperialism.* To the rising sun of Japan and to the setting sun of Churchill we oppose equally our own blood red banner of *revolt.* It is only under this banner, the banner of the revolutionary workers of the World, that Fascisms, whether it be Hitler's fascism or Churchill's, can be fought and done to death. It is the immediate and inescapable duty of you, our British comrades, towards the international working class, to overthrow your own Imperialist exploiters. A Workers' Britain, that is a Socialist Britain, will be the greatest blow to Hitler and his gang. A Revolution in Britain and America will flare up the revolutionary embers in France and the fire of the Revolution will urge the German and Italian workers to destroy their own oppressors.

Comrades! We have one common goal and one common enemy. Let us march forward together with the indomitable resolve to crush our bloodthirsty exploiters. Not all the forces of Hitler, Churchill and Tojo can prevail against the unconquerable might of the United Workers of the World.

DOWN WITH IMPERIALIST WAR! DOWN WITH ALL IMPERIALISM! DOWN WITH THE HIGH COMMAND AND THE OFFICER CASTE! COMPLETE FREEDOM OF SPEECH FOR SOLDIERS AND SAILORS! Organise soldiers' and sailors' committees! *For the Revolutionary Unity of Workers, Peasants, Soldiers and Sailors! For Peace and a Workers' Government!* LONG LIVE THE WORLD REVOLUTION.

Issued by:
The LANKA SAMA SAMAJA PARTY section of the BOLSHEVIK WORKERS' PARTY of India, Burma and Ceylon. (Fourth International)

20.4.42.

Please read and pass this on.

Appendix B

RAF and FLEET AIR ARM flying personnel who took part in the operations over Ceylon in April 1942.

Notes: (1) Although every effort has been made to identify airmen by their initials it has not proved possible, from available records, to do this in all cases.

(2) The list of Fleet Air Arm aircrew is incomplete. Squadrons were formed on a much less permanent basis than in the RAF and records are not comprehensive.

Rank	Name	Squadron	Remarks
P/O.	Abbott, A. W.	205	Killed
F/Lt.	Adcock, E.	11	South African. Killed
Sgt.	Alderton	11	
Sgt.	Allen, E. A.	205	Killed
Lt.	Allingham, P.	806	
F/O.	Allison, T. H. C.	30	Wounded
Sgt.	Anderson, C. W.	11	
P/O.	Annson, W. H.	11	Australian
S/Ldr.	Ault, K.	11	Killed
P/O.	Bayly, G. M.	413	
Cpl.	Bazzani	321	Dutch
Sub/Lt.	Beale, A. W. D., DSC	788	Killed
Sgt.	Bell, J. C. A.	11	Killed
Sgt.	Bennett, H.	413	
S/Ldr.	Birchall, L. J., DFC	413	Canadian. Prisoner of War
Sgt.	Bird ("Dickie")	240	
Cpl.	Blume	321	Dutch
Ldg. Naval Airman	Bolton, D.	788	Killed
Sgt.	Boltwood	11	
Sgt.	Bonfield	11	Australian
Sub/Lt.	Bonnell, F. W.	806	Killed
Sgt.	Bourke, P.	413	Killed

F/O.	Bourne, R. K.	413	Killed
F/Sgt.	Bowie, D. D. P.	261	Wounded
F/Lt.	Bradshaw, W., DFC	240	
P/O.	Brown, A.	258	
Sgt.	Brown	11	
Sgt.	Browne, O. J.	30	Killed
P/O.	Burgan, G. S., DFC	11	Killed
Sgt.	Burke	240	Killed
Sgt.	Calorossi, L. A.	413	Killed
Sgt.	Cameron	11	
F/Sgt.	Carlaw, A. D.	202	New Zealander
Sub/Lt.	Carter, D. R.	788	
P/O.	Cartwright, H. K.	30	Wounded
P/O.	Caswell, G. E.	30	Killed
Sgt.	Catlin, B.	413	Wounded. Prisoner of War
F/Sgt.	Charlton	240	
W/Cmdr.	Chater, G. F., DFC	30	South African
F/Lt.	Cleaver, R. B.	261	
F/O.	Cockton, J. R.	11	
Sgt.	Cole, L.	240	
Sgt.	Cook, W.	413	Wounded. Prisoner of War.
F/Sgt.	Cooper	240	
Sub/Lt.	Cope, I. E.	788	Wounded
Sgt.	Copsey	11	
F/O.	Counter, C. F.	261	
Lieut.	Cramer	321	Dutch
Sub/Lt.	Cranston, J. C. J.	814	Lost with H.M.S. *Hermes*
Sub/Lt.	Crease, G. H.	788	Australian. Wounded
Sgt.	Cruise	11	
Sgt.	Cubitt	11	
Cpl.	Daniells, A. T. E.	205	Killed
Sgt.	Davy, L. S.	413	
Sgt.	Davidson, I. N.	413	Killed
LAC.	Delmeyer	321	Dutch
Sgt.	Dingley	240	
Sgt.	Dodd, W. C. F.	205	Killed
F/O.	Donald, A. W.	11	Killed
Sgt.	Dreaver	240	
Cpl.	Duyts	321	Dutch
Sgt.	Eckersley, G. K.	11	Killed
P/O.	Evans	11	Killed

W/O.	Everett, A. D.	240	
S/Ldr.	Fletcher, P. C., DFC	258	Rhodesian. Wounded
LAC.	Fountain	240	
F/Lt.	Fulford, D., DFC	261	
P/O.	Gardner, C. J. T., OBE	240	
F/Sgt.	Garnham, R. K.	11	New Zealander
Sgt.	Garroway, P. H.	413	
F/Sgt.	Gauthier, C. J.	261	Wounded
Sgt.	Gavin, L. P.	258	
P/O.	Geffene, D.	30	American. Killed
Sgt.	Gilmore, H. G.	11	
Lieut.	Girvin, E. C.	11	South African
F/Lt.	Graham, J. R.	205	Killed
Sgt.	Gray, M.C.	11	Killed
F/O.	Gregg, A. M.	273	Killed
LAC.	Griffiths	240	
Sgt.	Gunn	240	
F/Sgt.	Gurney, G. C.	413	Killed
P/O.	Hall, R. G.	261	
Lieut.	Hamers	321	Dutch
Sgt.	Harper, J. K.	413	Killed
Sgt.	Harris	240	
Petty Officer	Heath	788	
Sgt.	Henzell, J.	413	Killed
F/O.	Hervey, R. G.	413	Canadian. Killed
Cpl.	Heynaker	321	Dutch
F/Lt.	Hildyard, D. H. T.	205	
Sub/Lt.	Hinton, R. V.	803	
Sgt.	Hocking	11	
Sgt.	Holf, J.	413	
Sgt.	Hooper, J. K.	413	Canadian. Killed
Sub/Lt.	Hordern, M.	806	
Sgt.	Hore, L. A.	11	
Sgt.	Housley, D. L.	413	Killed
W/O.	Howe, T. W. A.	11	
P/O.	Hudson, W.	11	Australian
Sub/Lt.	Jacob, R. F. H.	803	Killed
Naval Air-man	Johnson	806	
F/O.	Kenny, P. N.	413	Prisoner of War
P/O.	Knight, R.	11	South African. Killed

Cpl.	Knip	321	Dutch
F/Lt.	Leach, H. D. T.	205	Killed
S/Ldr.	Lewis, A. G., DFC	261	Wounded
Sgt.	Lewis	240	
LAC.	Lewis	205	Killed
F/Lt.	Lockhart, J.	258	Killed
Sgt.	Lockwood, G.	261	
Lieut.	Longsdon, S. M. de L.	788	Wounded
Sgt.	Lunn	240	
Sgt.	McAuley, L. E.	11	Killed
Sgt.	McCann	11	
Lt.	McEwan, B.	803	
Sgt.	McLennan	11	Killed
P/O.	Macdonald, D. A.	30	Australian
P/O.	Macdonald, D. K.	30	Canadian
F/Lt.	McFadden, A.	258	Killed
Sgt.	McFadzean, A.	11	
Sub/Lt.	Mackay, N.R.	788	
Sgt.	Mann, K. A. S.	261	
Sgt.	Markham	413	Killed
Sub/Lt.	Marshall, E.	806	
F/Lt.	Marshall, J. V.	261	
F/Sgt.	Martin, J. D.	261	
W/O.	Mason, F.	11	
P/O.	Matheson, W. R.	11	
P/O.	Mayes, R.	261	
Sub/Lt.	Meakin, P. A.	788	Wounded
P/O.	Milnes, A. H.	258	
Sgt.	Missett	240	
Sgt.	Moore, M. G.	11	
Sgt.	Moorhouse, K. N.	258	
LAC.	Morgan	240	
Sgt.	Moxham, J. D.	413	South African. Killed
P/O.	Neill, R. N.	258	Killed
Sgt.	Nell, F. J. G.	11	Killed
P/O.	Nicholls, D. B. F.	258	
Sgt.	Noney	202	
F/Sgt.	Oliver	240	
W/O.	Onyette, G. C.	413	Canadian. Prisoner of War.
AC.	Osborne	240	
F/Sgt.	Ovens, L. A., DFM	30	Killed

P/O.	Paterson, J. M. K.	240	
F/Sgt.	Paxton, T. G.	30	Killed
Sgt.	Payne, P. L.	11	
Sub/Lt.	Peace, A.	806	Killed
F/Lt.	Peacock-Edwards, S. R., DFC	258	Rhodesian. Wounded.
Sgt.	Pearce, W. E.	261	Killed
Sub/Lt.	Peirano, P. R.	273	Killed
Sub/Lt.	Pettitt, K. J. M.	806	Killed
Sgt.	Phillips, F. C.	413	Wounded. Prisoner of War
Cpl.	Pieschel	321	Dutch
Sgt.	Porter	240	
Lieut.	Pountney, C. A.	788	Australian. Wounded
Sgt.	Prentice	240	
Sgt.	Rawnsley, L. T.	261	Wounded
F/Sgt.	Redmond	240	
F/Sgt.	Rigby	11	
F/Lt.	Roberts, O. G. E.	413	
Sgt.	Robins	240	
F/O.	Round, A.	240	
F/Lt.	Sharp, D. J. T., DFC	258	New Zealander
Sub/Lt.	Shaw, C. T.	788	
Sub/Lt.	Sinclair	806	
Sgt.	Singleton	202	
Naval Airman	Skingley, G.	788	Killed
F/O.	Smith, H. T. L.	11	
P/O.	Smith, P. F.	11	
Sgt.	Smith, H. J.	413	
W/Cmdr.	Smyth, A. J. M., DFC	11	
Sgt.	Stevenson, N. L.	11	Killed
Sgt.	Sutton	11	
Sub/Lt.	Sykes, J. H. C.	806	
Sgt.	Taylor, A.	413	
Sgt.	Thain, R. N.	258	Killed
F/Lt.	Thomas, R., DFC	413	South African. Killed
Sgt.	Travers, A. R.	11	Killed
P/O.	Tremlett, E. M. T.	258	Killed
Cpl.	van Zweiten	321	Dutch
Lieut.	Venema	321	Dutch
P/O.	Vineberg, A.	413	

Sgt.	Visser	321	Dutch
Sgt.	Walker, R. D.	205	Killed
Sgt.	Walton, J. W.	261	Killed
Sgt.	Walmsley	240	
F/Sgt.	Warnick, A. T.	261	
Sgt.	Westby	240	
Sgt.	Whiles, S. D.	11	Killed
P/O.	White, C. C.	258	
Sub/Lt.	White-Smith, I. K.	803	Killed
Sgt.	Whittaker	258	
Sgt.	Wixted, T. J.	11	
Cpl.	Zuycham	321	Dutch

Bibliography

Agar, Captain Augustus, VC, RN: *Footprints in the Sea* (Evans Bros.)
Bateson, Charles; *The War with Japan* (Barrie & Ratcliff)
Bryant, Sir Arthur; *The Turn of the Tide* (Collins) – 1957
Churchill, Sir Winston S.; *The Second World War* (Cassell) – 1948-54.
Coughlin, Tom; *The Dangerous Sky* (William Kimber)
Crawley, Aiden; *De Gaulle* (Collins)
Donahue, Arthur; *Last Flight From Singapore* (Macmillan) – 1944
Fuchida, Captain Mitsuo; *Midway, the Battle that Doomed Japan* (Hutchinson)
Gibson, Wing Commander Guy, VC, DSO, DFC; *Enemy Coast Ahead* (Michael Joseph) – 1946
Harris, Marshal of the RAF Sir Arthur T.; GCB, OBE, AFC, Ll.D; *Bomber Offensive* (Collins) – 1947
Hezlett, Vice Admiral Sir Arthur, KBE, CB, DSO, D.Sc; *Aircraft and Sea Power* (Peter Davies)
Kirby, Major General Sir Woodburn & Others; *History of the Second World War – The War against Japan* (H.M. Stationery Office) – 1957-65
Leasor, James: *Singapore* (Houghton & Stoughton)
Lithgow, Mike; *Mach One* (Allan Wingate) – 1954
Lockwood, Douglas; *Australia's Pearl Harbour* (Cassell, Australia)
Lord, Walter; *Day of Infamy* (Hamish Hamilton) – 1957
  Incredible Victory, The Battle of Midway (Hamish Hamilton)
MacIntyre, Captain Donald, DSO, DSC, RN; *Fighting Admiral* (Evans Bros)
Millot, Bernard; *Divine Thunder* (Macdonald)
Morison, Samuel Elliott; *History of United States Naval Operations in*

World War II. (Little Brown & Co.) 1947-62

Okumiya, Masutake and Horikoshi, Jiro; *Zero* (Dutton) – 1957

Potter, John Deane; *Admiral of the Pacific, the Life of Yamamoto* (Heinemann)

Roskill, Captain S. W., RN; *A Merchant Fleet at War* (Collins) *History of the Second World War – The War at Sea. Vol II* (H. M. Stationery Office) 1956–61

Russell, Lord (of Liverpool); *Knights of Bushido* (Cassell)

Russell, Wing Commander Wilfred W.; *Forgotten Skies* (Hutchinson)

Sadler, A. L.; *A Short History of Japan* (Faber & Faber) – 1963

Skidmore, Ian; *Escape from the Rising Sun* (Leo Cooper)

Slim, Field Marshal Sir William, GCB, DSO, MC; *Defeat into Victory* (Cassell) – 1956

Turner, L. C. F., Gordon-Cumming, H. R., Betzler, J. E.; *War in the Southern Oceans 1939-45* (Oxford University Press)

War History No. 26; (Japanese Defence Agency)

The author would like to thank the Controller of H.M. Stationery Office for permission to quote from *The War at Sea;* Messrs. Heinemann for *Admiral of the Pacific: The Life of Yamamoto;* Messrs. Evans for *Footprints of the Sea:* Messrs. Cassell for *The Second World War,* Messrs. Dutton for *Zero* and Marshal of the Royal Air Force Sir Arthur Harris for *Bomber Offensive.*

Index

(Ranks are the last known)